AF322667

BLESSING OR BURDEN
Taking Care Of Your Elderly

BLESSING OR BURDEN
Taking Care Of Your Elderly

Written By
Chioma Modest Chime

Copyright 2024 by Chioma Modest Chime

All rights reserved. In accordance with the U.S. Copyright Act of 1976, the scanning, uploading, and electronic sharing of any part of this book without permission of the publisher constitute unlawful piracy and theft of the author's intellectual property. If you would like to use material from the book (other than for review purposes), prior written permission must be obtained.

Thank you for your support of the author's rights.

The publisher assisted in file preparation, i.e., editing, typesetting, cover design, etc. and is not responsible for the content within this book, websites, or social media pages (or their content) related to this publication.

Hardback ISBN: 979-8-8692-8665-9
Paperback ISBN: 979-8-8692-6905-8
E-Book: 979-8-8692-6906-5

Published in United States of America 10 9 8 7 6 5 4 3 2 1

Table of Contents

Introduction

'Blessing or Burden' is a fictional work that intricately weaves together narratives from multiple real-life events, offering a profound exploration of caregiving for the elderly. As each chapter unfolds with diverse voices, styles, and tones, the collective accounts poignantly highlight the complexities and joys of providing care and compassion to our older loved ones. This well coordinated effort sheds light on the nuances of familial relationships, urging readers to embrace empathy, understanding, and love in the face of challenges and differences.

I.

CHAPTER 1
How It All Started

It was a lovely Saturday afternoon, the beginning of fall, and the weather was perfect for a picnic or a walk in the park. Instead of that, I invited some of my friends over to my house for a little get-together and chat with the ladies. We haven't done this in a while, not since COVID; we used to take turns hosting the group on weekends before the pandemic. Since then, it has been hard for us to gather the way we used to because of life, work, and family changes.

My mother has been living with me since my father passed away in 2018. She visits my other siblings but always comes right back to my house, where she has her room, space, and other things. She is elderly and retired, and I feel blessed to still have her around, especially since my dad is no longer with us. I have relations, colleagues, and friends who either do not know their parents or lost them at an early age. One of my friends was a baby when her mother passed away, and her father did not want her. She grew up in an orphanage and did not know what it means or how it feels to have parents or watch them grow old. I know that there are a lot of people like her, which is why I feel blessed to have my mother around.

While my friends were at my house, my mom came downstairs to the kitchen to grab some things and greeted my friends. They were all excited to meet her. After she went back upstairs, we started talking about the elderly. Some of the topics we discussed were elder abuse, isolation, neglect, and abandonment. We all had different stories to tell about the elderly. I reminded them about the fifth commandment that states that we should honor our mother and father; it is actually the only commandment that came with a promise (so that your days will be long). I told them about a viral video from the previous year about a young lady who beat her elderly mother with a stick because she had a bladder accident. The lady made her mother bathe herself with very cold water, not knowing that her neighbor who had witnessed all the abuses recorded it and shared it with a bunch of people. The community saw the video, rescued the elderly woman from her daughter, and appropriately punished the daughter.

Our discussion led me to the Scriptures, where it said in Psalm 71:9 "Do not cast me away when I am old; do not forsake me when my strength is gone." In Proverbs chapter 30 vs 17, the Scripture says that the eyes that mock a father and despise a mother's instructions will be plucked out by ravens of the valley and eaten by vultures. In other words, do not despise your parents especially when they are older, as there are consequences. Although some people seem not to care about the consequences of dishonoring and disregarding their elderly parents.

The above scriptures drew my attention to a story of a young girl who was raised by her single mother. Her mother sold most of her expensive jewelry and clothing to put her through school. When she graduated and got a well-paying job that helped her travel out of the country, she started having a series of problems. She was fired from her job for something she knew nothing about. When she arrived in the new country, she decided to stay and get her permit there. It took longer than expected, and she faced depression and a bunch of issues, with some days hardly finding something to eat.

Sometimes, when people are in need or going through difficult times, that's when they remember God. She started going to all sorts of pastors to pray for her. During one of her visits to these pastors, one of them told her that her mother had bewitched her and that she needed to cut ties with her mother; otherwise, things would be harder for her. She stopped talking to her mother for almost ten years. When she realized that things were not going as she had anticipated, she decided to seek a different pastor's opinion. This pastor prayed for her and told her that until she made peace with her mother, things would never be better for her. She told the pastor how her mother had bewitched her and blocked all her progress. The pastor told her that the vision he had seen showed him that her mother was never a witch or evil but had been constantly praying for her well-being, even though she had not talked to her in years.

This pastor reconciled her with her mother, and they could not have been happier. She maintained a very good and strong relationship with her mother until she was gone. After the reconciliation, things started falling into place for her. She is now married with three children. The power of motherly love and blessings.

There was another story that went viral and got me crying my eyes out. This elderly woman was caught sleeping in her truck by police officers who had kept getting phone calls about a woman who had been sleeping in her vehicle for days. When they got to her, she told them that she had been kicked out of her son's house by her own son. She had been a homemaker when she was younger and had children. Her husband never let her do any job. When her husband died, she had to go live with her son, who was married at the time. She thought that she was helping around the house, but her daughter-in-law felt like she was in the way. It created a big marital problem between the son and his wife, who threatened to leave the marriage if he did not send his mother out of the house. He asked his mother to leave the house; he did not care how old his mother was or what the weather was like. It was in the middle of winter, and this old woman was sleeping in her car without any food or water. She did not want to go back to her son's house because she did not want to be the cause of their marital problems. The son did not even think to put her in a home. He completely forgot how she carried him in her womb, nourished and protected him for nine whole months; took care of him until he was old enough to get a job and make his own family. And he could not think of anything to do with her but throw her out of the house because his wife was not getting along with his mother.

CHAPTER 2
My Grandmother

I grew up in a culture where taking care of the elderly was regarded as an important duty, and it was expected that you would care for them even better than they did for you when you were younger. In our community, nursing homes and assisted living were unfamiliar concepts. If your elderly parents were not living with you or not being checked on regularly, the community elders would reach out to inquire why you were not fulfilling your obligations.

Before my grandfather passed away, he and my grandmother lived in their country home. They often had one or two grandchildren staying with them for certain periods or during school breaks. They always treated all their grandchildren equally and looked out for us, imparting knowledge about our tradition and culture, teaching us responsibility, and encouraging us to look out for each other.

My grandfather worked with the coal corporation, while my grandmother, who was a homemaker, took care of everyone who walked through their door. She was an excellent cook, preparing various traditional dishes that were irresistible. In their spare time, they cultivated their own food, sometimes giving away produce to neighbors or selling them at the local market. They also raised livestock, and I cherished visiting them during harvest.

After my grandfather's passing, my grandmother chose to remain in their country home. Concerned about her well-being, we visited often and made sure she received medical attention when necessary. As she grew older and was unable to live in their country home alone, she rotated among her children's houses, where they took turns caring for her.

Despite her age, she engaged with each grandchild according to their age and was a youthful soul and a peacemaker. I recall an incident when I had a disagreement with my mother and refused to eat for several days to show my deep hurt. When my grandmother learned of this, she paid us a visit, serving her food and inviting me to eat with her. She recognized the food she had prepared as one of my favorites and refused to accept my excuse for not eating it. This led to a heartfelt conversation where she helped resolve the conflict between my mother and me, ultimately encouraging me to eat and bringing peace to the situation.

She was beloved by everyone. I remember one time when she was experiencing abdominal pain. She went to the local hospital and was diagnosed with appendicitis, which is the inflammation of the appendix causing a lot of pain. She was transferred to another hospital where they had the staff and resources for the type of surgery she needed. She was admitted at the general hospital where she had the surgery. During her stay at the hospital, she received tremendous love and care from the entire hospital staff.

The funny part of her hospital stay was when every member of my family, spanning from my grandfather, parents, uncles, aunties, and cousins, young and old, would all be at the hospital. Even the ones living in different states came when they heard she was in the hospital. It became so overwhelming that the hospital staff had to call security to send us out of the unit. However, that did not stop us from being there every day from morning till evening. All the staff knew us by name because we were always in their way. None of us wanted to miss out; I was so little back then but I still remember how my aunties were basically fighting over who would care for her more.

When she got discharged from the hospital, the staff were sad that she was leaving but happy that they would not have to deal with my family anymore. After the fight over whose house she should go to, she told all of us that she loved us so much but would prefer to go back to her own house. As soon as that decision was made, we all decided that we would go with her to her country house. She refused and said that she could only allow two people to come with her. It was a very difficult decision to make, but they agreed that my two youngest aunties and my eldest sister would stay with her until she fully recovered and was back to her normal routine.

She appreciated all of us for being at the hospital with her throughout her stay. We went every weekend to visit her until she was back on her feet. Whenever my grandmother would go to stay at any of my aunties or uncles' homes, we would visit them often because we always liked to be around her, except for when she would travel out of the state. In that case, we would constantly be in contact to know when she would be back. It was a great blessing caring for her when she reached a point in her life where she could not care for herself. Even at that point, she was still fighting to be independent.

I remember one incident where she had a bowel accident while staying with us. My elder sister was helping her with her bath because she was sick and weak and was not able to do it herself. My sister offered to wash her undergarment, but she refused, stating that she had been washing her undergarments herself and was still capable of doing so. My sister explained to her that she had a bowel accident and might not wash it well due to her ailment, but she insisted and started crying and praying to God to come and take her if she had reached the point of having bowel accidents.

We tried to explain to her that when you get to a certain age, you might need some help from people around even though you think you are still capable of doing everything by yourself. She looked at us and asked what age that might be because she had not gotten to that age yet. Meanwhile, she was eighty-four. She died the following year, at eighty-five. She was sick and in the hospital, I cannot remember what it was, but most of her grandchildren were staying in the hospital with her. We were taking turns.

That fateful day, we were all around her, chatting with each other and asking her questions. After a few hours, she asked us to give her some time to rest and requested that we should all go outside her room and continue our conversations. We did as she requested. A few minutes later, we saw the nurse go into the room, followed by a doctor. We became curious when the doctor came to us and told us that she had peacefully passed away in her sleep. It was heartbreaking for us, even though we knew that she was ready; we were not ready for her to go yet.

She did not want us to see her pass on, which is why she sent us all out of the room. We mourned her, but we knew that she had a peaceful transition, which gave us consolation and closure. Our lives changed after she passed on. Some of us started to aspire to be like her. She was a great role model, missed by all, and it was a huge blessing caring for her.

CHAPTER 3
Nora's Account
Taking Care of Mom

You know, growing up, our mom was something else. My sisters and I saw her as our modern-day Margaret Thatcher. She had this air of strictness about her that made us feel like she had no time for our childish antics. We, three sisters, used to wonder if she even liked us, let alone loved us. She had all these rules and expectations that we felt suffocated by. You dare not argue with or disobey any of her rules because there would be a great consequence.

Bedtimes were non-negotiable. She had a set time for you to be done with your schoolwork, chores, get things ready for the next day, and be in bed at the appointed time. Eating vegetables was inevitable and had to be devoured before dessert. Our house had to be spotless all the time. If you ventured to make a mess as a child or leave something where it was not supposed to be, you might not live to tell your story. It was like living in a military regime, and we often whispered to each other, "What's up with Mom?" "Why did she have us if she did not like or want children?" We felt unwanted and unloved.

As we got older, we started pushing back. Arguments would erupt over curfews, our clothing choices, and the music we listened to. We desperately wanted a mom who would just listen to us, understand our desires, and maybe even smile occasionally. But that just wasn't her. What we didn't realize then was that mom had her reasons. She had seen the world's rough edges and wanted to shield us from its hardships. She genuinely believed that her discipline and structure were the keys to our success.

I remember one occasion where my younger sister, a teenager back then dressed to go hang out with her friends. She wore a short dress with a little bare back, she got to the living room to tell our mom that she was going to her friends. She looked her up and down and asked her when she would be going. She answered that she was about to leave. Mom simply said to her, "go put on some clothes, you cannot go out naked." My sister insisted that she had some clothes on. Mom got up to inspect what cloth she had and yanked the short dress off her by ripping it. My sister ran to the room naked, crying. There goes mom right behind her yelling and screaming at her on top of her voice saying that she was planning on getting herself pregnant at a young age. She stated that if she went out dressed like that, it would attract pervs who would easily rip her cloth off and devour her innocence. She went on and told her that she should dress how she wanted to be addressed. I understood what she was trying to do but her method was way off. My younger sister ended up not going out that evening because she was very upset.

Another incident was when I had my friends from school over at the house, mom came out to the living room to assess them. A few minutes later, she called me to her room and demanded that I ask two of those friends to leave. When I asked her what they did wrong, she told me that they were not from a responsible family, that they did not get proper home training. I did not know how to tell my visitors to leave because of what my mom thinks of them. I did not want her to come out and tell them to leave herself so I decided to tell them that it would be best to take our chat to a different location. One of my friends agreed for us to come to her house. Mom was eavesdropping on our conversation; she called me and said that I was not going anywhere with them. I just walked out of her room and was ready to leave with my friends when I felt a very hot slap on my right cheek. My friends literally ran out of the house. I was so embarrassed; I couldn't say anything because I had tears rolling down my cheeks. My friends could not stay at my house, and I could not go anywhere with them. "What kind of life is this?" I asked myself. The only thing she said to me was that I shouldn't have defied her or her orders. She went ahead and said to me, "one day you all will understand why I am doing what I'm doing."

Years went by, and we grew into adults, got married, and started our own families. It's then that we began to see the values in our mom's teachings, even though she approached it in a way we found challenging. We realized that her strictness played a significant role in shaping us into responsible, disciplined individuals with strong work, life, and social ethics. While we may not have had a typical mother-daughter bond, we now understand that she would always stand up for us and fight for our best interests.

Mom's keen judgment of character became evident when I encountered the first man who came to ask for my hand in marriage. I was smitten with him, believing his declarations of love and familiarity. Despite our restrictions on opposite-sex friendships, I engaged in a secret relationship with him for about three months. When the time came for him to meet my parents, Mom interrogated him intensely, acting as the voice of the family. She astutely observed his behavior and questioned his intentions, leaving me conflicted but prepared for the aftermath.

After he left, Mom sat me down and imparted invaluable advice on self-protection. She probed about the extent of my acquaintance with him, unearthing unsettling truths about his involvement in illegal activities and existing marital ties. Though I initially defended his character, Mom's guidance prompted me to confront him with her questions. Her foresight proved accurate when he revealed his deceit, exposing his marital status and hidden family.

This revelation marked a turning point for my sisters and me, as we recognized the depth of our mother's care and concern. Our initial desire to distance ourselves from her shifted as we matured, understanding the significance of her "tough" love. Despite our earlier intentions to establish independence, we now embraced her protective nature and acknowledged the wisdom in her actions.

As our father's passing and Mom's declining health reshaped our family dynamics, we collectively accepted and appreciated her unique expression of love. Although challenging at times, we acknowledged the importance of honoring and respecting her authority, recognizing her unwavering devotion to our well-being. With gratitude, we navigated her quirks and idiosyncrasies, fostering a closer familial bond built on acceptance and unconditional love.

Caring for Mom in her old age became a sacred duty and privilege, allowing us to repay her years of love and sacrifice. Embracing our roles as devoted daughters, we cherished every moment with her, recognizing her indomitable spirit and enduring influence. Rather than seeking to

change her, we embraced her for who she is
– a strict yet loving matriarch – and found
solace in her enduring presence in our lives.

We continue to pray for Mom's well-being,
treasuring each day spent with her and
expressing gratitude for the lessons she
imparted. Despite our perceptions in our
youth, caring for her is now a source of joy
and fulfillment, underscoring the depth of
our enduring love and appreciation for her
unwavering guidance. Mom remains the
cornerstone of our family, a beacon of
strength and love, and we are forever
grateful for her presence in our lives.

CHAPTER 4

Daniel's Account
Caring for My Elderly Parents

I am what people would call 'born by mistake' lol. My three siblings were born several years before I was conceived. My parents were on vacation celebrating their 25th wedding anniversary when my mother got pregnant with me. My immediate elder brother was 20 years older than me, that would tell you how old my other siblings are. I have two older brothers and one older sister.

When I was in middle school, my siblings were all out of the house; so, I was left with my parent. By the time I was in high school, they were old. I was well taken care of, but I was upset at them for having me real late. I felt like I was their 'after thought'.

They loved me so dearly to the point that we became each other's best friend. I barely go anywhere. I did not have friends. Some people thought that I was anti-social, but I know myself; I socialize with my parents who were so worried about me that if I go out with friends, they will keep calling my phone until I get home.

We lived on a farm, my parents owned and cared for the farm. We had a lot of farm animals, and I could not help but assist them in caring for the animals and the farm. It was always the three of us, though during the holidays like Thanksgiving, Christmas, Easter, and other holidays, everyone would come over to the house for the holiday feast.

After high school, I decided that I would go to a college that is very close to home so that I would not have to leave my parents by themselves. I had gotten so used to them that it started affecting my social life. Each time I tried to go out with my friends, it would always end up in me hurrying back home leaving my friends out there.

Our closeness became so scary because it was also affecting them. They used to vacation a lot but with me in the house with them they barely go out. They would order food and eat in during special events like anniversaries. I tried several times to make them go out on their special days like birthdays or anniversaries, but they would refuse to go. I don't know if they were afraid that they might get pregnant again on vacation like they did with me.

While living with my parents, I became a big brother to my nieces and nephews. They trusted me with all their secrets; they were always open with me. One of my nephews had a same-sex partner and did not know how to come out to the family, he confided in me, and I helped him through the process. This relationship that I have with my nieces and nephews extended to their children after they got married and had their own children.

A few years after I graduated from college and started working while still living with and helping my parent with the farm work, my father passed away; that broke my mom. My father was never sick, did not like going to providers for medical checkups. He complained of a little pain in his groin area and that the pain was making it difficult for him to urinate. We all thought that it was urinary tract infection (UTI). He did not want to go see a provider because he believed in natural cures for everything, so he decided that he would take some cranberry juice and some local herbs. He always had herbs for everything from headache, heartburn, to some severe health issues. He never believed in modern medicines. He was what you would call a naturalist; even with the farm animals, he would always use natural remedies for them.

When his pain and discomfort would not go away after more than a week, we had to make him go to a doctor which he dreaded. That day was the longest day of our lives especially for me. My brothers went with us to the doctor because they knew the doctor. He was constantly giving them updates on my father's health, I was very devastated to even listen to what the doctor was saying but I knew that it was bad.

My Mom was asked to stay home against her wish because they went everywhere together except for when my dad was working. Oh, I forgot the part that he asked my mom not to work while he worked and provided for the family. My Mom never lacked anything. As a matter of fact, she was the envy of the other women because she always looked like a million-dollar princess. While at the hospital, my phone was blowing off from my mom calling to see how everything was going and to see if she needed to come over there.

My dad was diagnosed with prostate cancer that had metastasized to his bones and some vital organs. There was nothing much that the doctors could do for him. They referred us to a hematologist/oncologist who recommended chemotherapy and radiation, but my dad declined it and said that he had lived a good life and was ready to go. We weighed the benefits and the risk of those treatments and decided to honor my dad's decision.

I was devastated because I was hoping to have more time with him, though he was already very old. As soon as dad got home from the hospital, he went from vibrant to frail. He started looking sickly and lost interest in things that he would normally jump at. My Mom was on the verge of being depressed as a result of this. I had my siblings coming to help occasionally, but his care was completely on me. I took a family medical leave from my work to be able to care for him full time.

When he passed away, our lives were shattered, but we needed to be strong for my mom who was not doing too well as a result of my Dad's health condition. After my Dad's funeral, Mom became so fragile and aged drastically. I believe that she went into a brief depression. Her care fell solely on me just like my dad's since I was the only one still living with them. Because of what happened to my dad, my siblings and I decided that my mom, in addition to going to her primary care physician, would be going to get checked out regularly.

I know that you might be wondering why I have not mentioned a wife or girlfriend, well, I don't have either one and I am not gay. When I graduated from college, I was offered a job outside our state, but I declined it because by then my parents were already too old to be left by themselves to manage a big family farm. So, I decided that I was going to apply for jobs within. I became so close and attached to them that I could not live without them. Caring for them and helping with the farm work was very time-consuming, and I never even thought about a social life. I tried to date, but none of the dates worked out, so I decided to put a hold on the dating life. I know that you might be thinking that I put my life on hold to care for my parent, but I did not put my life on hold, and no one forced me to do it; in fact, I was happy doing it. What's funny is that I was not only taking care of my parents but other family members.

Four years after my dad passed away, my mom's health started failing. She started getting sick constantly; from minor doctor's visits to major hospital stays. I had to request an early retirement from my job because of constant calling outs, applying for several family medical leaves. At a point, I was taking her everywhere I went, even to work sometimes because I did not trust her to not fall or get into a health crisis while by herself. She had already started having falls here and there. Mom had very bad arthritis that limited her mobility and was supposed to be wheelchair-bound, but she lived in denial and would want to walk and end up falling. Despite her health issues, mom was still in her right mind and always wanted to be in control of everything around her. We were constantly fighting because she would not listen to my instructions, as all her married life, she had always been the decision-maker and she still saw me as her little baby boy.

I changed the layout of our farm home to be more wheelchair friendly, and I got her an electric wheelchair so that she would be able to wheel herself around the farm without hurting herself. She loved working on the farm; she would wheel herself to where she had a flower garden to care for her plants. She took care of our farm animals like they were humans; she would carry conversations with the dogs and sometimes the goats. I displayed what you would call a "tough love" towards her. People who don't know us would think that I was being mean to her, but that was the only way that I could get her to do the right things for her safety and well-being.

Since I couldn't go anywhere without my mom, I took her with me to work on several occasions, and it was not the best plan. We had caregivers come to the house to stay with her, but she got worse with each caregiver. Since dad passed away, she became a grumpy old lady and would not listen to anyone. Because of these, I retired to stay with her.

Her health kept declining by the day, her memory started to decline as well. She got to a point where she would carry a full conversation with an invisible person. When you ask her who she was talking to, she would mention my dad's name and tell you that he would not listen to anything she was saying. One of the days, she told me that she was asking my dad if she could come with him. I remember asking her where she was wanting to go with him; she responded that she was not sure but that my dad looked good and much younger than her. By this time, I knew that she was getting ready to go but I was not ready for her to go because it felt like I would be lost and alone in this world without her. It was bad enough that I lost my dad; losing her was unthinkable.

The day that mom passed away was the worst day of my life. I had an argument with her the night before because she would not eat her food. She just said that she was not hungry because she was waiting for my dad to come get her. I started explaining to her that dad has been dead a while now and would not come and get her. She insisted that I did not know what I was talking about because he promised to come get her. I decided to play along with her; I told her that if she did not eat that dad would not come to get her. That got about three to four bites of food in her stomach.

After she took her medications, she refused

to go to sleep because she was waiting on her husband, but she agreed to lay in her bed and wait. During the night, I went to her room to check on her, but she was already sleeping, so I just covered her with her quilt and left her door ajar so that I would hear her when she calls for help. Around 4 AM, I got up to go check on her because usually she would call for me to take her to the bathroom around that time. When I got to her room, she was in the same position from the last time I checked on her.

I went to her to wake her up, but she was already gone. I called the emergency team because I did not want to believe that she would just leave me by myself. They came and tried to resuscitate her, but she was already gone, but they took her to the hospital anyways because I insisted. We got to the emergency department and the ER doctor pronounced her dead. I lost it; I wailed like a baby. I kept shaking her gently to see if I could wake her up, but I couldn't because she was gone. My mom left me alone and by myself in this wicked world.

So, you were asking if it was a blessing or a burden to care for my parent. I will not say that it was a burden, I'll say that I was obligated to do so judging by the conditions surrounding my birth and their age and health conditions. I loved them so dearly and miss them. I know that they have both reunited with each other and hope to see them soon. I mean whenever God calls me to him.

CHAPTER 5

Precious' Account
Taking Care of My Father Was Absolutely a
Huge Blessing For Me

My father was the best human created by God. He was a very kind, faithful, happy, generous human. Every good quality you can find in any human was abundant in my father. He loved his children equally, but being his first child/daughter, I always feel the unconditional love he had for me that I am sure was only meant for just me. Even when he will be forced to be angry at me, he will always do that with so much love. He was always patient with all of us. He was that kind of person who would always make a huge impact on everyone he came across. He was a God-fearing, peaceful, trustworthy, understanding, and worthy man.

My father took care of my siblings and me exceptionally well and likewise other people. He made sure we never lacked anything. He was the human definition of that father figure in the family. He made sure we were raised knowing what is wrong and what is right. He taught us to treat everyone with utmost respect. He inculcated in us the importance of integrity. He taught us to always be truthful in all our dealings and that honesty is the most important virtue.

When I talk about him taking care of my siblings and I, and other people, I mean that we had a lot of people living with us from when I was little until I got married and left the house. He never stopped helping people especially the less privileged ones. I lost count of people that he paid their tuitions from elementary to at least high school. I know a few of them that he paid their tuitions through college. He always put people first before himself. I will never forget how whenever we traveled to the country for Christmas celebration, he would have people come to the house to take their share of whatever he would pack up for them. It would range from bags of rice, meat, peas, tomatoes, onions, milk etc. It got to a point it became like a tradition. People look forward to it. Doing that gave him a kind of fulfillment that one cannot comprehend. Giving was his source of joy. He felt connected with people that he encountered.

Being all these great does not mean that he

did not punish us whenever we did something bad. He had his special way of punishing or disciplining us. After he accidentally hurt my little brother out of anger, he changed his method and never used any kind of violent approach. Father's method of disciplining is to sit you down and calmly talk sense into you to the point that you will never think of misbehaving again. He never raised his hands on us except for the one time with my little brother and he never raised his voice or yelled at anyone of us. He would give you all scenarios of how what you did was wrong and how it would be worse if you do not change your way of doing things.

I remember an incident that happened when I was a teenager. My Dad noticed that there was a particular boy who was always sneaking around our house hoping to get my attention. Truth be told, I also liked that young boy. I would seek every excuse to go to the front yard, so to get an opportunity to talk to the boy. To my surprise, I did not know that dad noticed us. One day, dad came back from work and called me to his room. One of my younger siblings wanted to go to dad's room with me and dad told her to go back to the living room that he needed to see just me. I knew then that I was in trouble, so I started making up logical excuses in my head why I went to the front yard earlier when I should've been doing my homework. I was wondering who told him that I went to the front yard, he just returned from work.

By the time we got to his room, I was ready to lie about checking to see if he was about to drive in, so I became calm and ready to prove my excuse. Dad sat down and asked me to sit beside him. Now, I was getting confused; he reached into his work bag and pulled out a book. He gave the book to me and asked me when I thought I could finish reading it because I will have to discuss the book with him and tell him the lesson I learned from the book. I looked at the volume of the book and told him that I will finish it before he comes back from work the next day. I loved reading story books then; he knew I could do it. He said, "ok, we will discuss tomorrow then"; He told me that was all. I was so relieved.

I started reading immediately after dinner, and I did not drop the book until I finished it at about 3 am in the morning, I lost track of time because of how interesting the book was. I barely slept before school in the morning. I was so quite all day and could not believe what I read from the book.

When Dad came home from work that evening, I was still so quiet and somber. He asked if I was ready to discuss the book, and I said yes. Dad asked if I was okay because of how quiet I was. I responded yes, and he inquired if I would like to start the discussion.

The very first thing that came out of my mouth was that I will not let teenage boys deceive me. In fact, I will not let any man sweet-talk me into losing my virginity until I am ready to bear the consequences of being impregnated. I started crying. The book is titled "Undesirable Element". It was about a young and very beautiful teenage girl. This beautiful teenage girl fell for a young boy's flattering and promises. She gave in and let the young man de-virgin her and got her pregnant. The young man denied having sex with her and joined the other young men to make fun of the young lady.

Where I grew up, teen pregnancy was a taboo, highly frowned down on. The young lady attempted committing suicide; she could not continue to go to school, her family disowned her. She went through it and had her baby, begging for food on the street.

Dad asked me to stop crying and just learn from what happened to the young girl in the book. That was the last day I snuck around trying to catch that young boy's attention.

I read that book when I was a teenager, and the lesson I learned from it helped me navigate my young age until I got married. I am in my sixties and still remember the story in that book. That was how Dad redirected me and brought awareness to me. He gave meaningful advice without making you feel bad or less of yourself. He would never argue with you on what is right or wrong or how best to do something, but he would calmly in a different way from what you would anticipate shift your thought and reasoning to the right thing. I loved my dad beyond what words can express. A man of peace.

I remember sometimes when he would argue with our Mom about irrelevant things, he would be the one to go to her and apologize. My Mom is a typical woman who would look to fight about things that are not there. My dad spoiled her with so much love and was always making sure that she was ok. He was constantly looking at her face to ensure that she was always happy. Any little frown from my Mom would get my dad worried.

Whenever they had any argument, we would all support him, and that usually would get my mom upset, and my dad would get livid with us asking us who appointed us judge. He would always tell us that the fight between a husband and a wife is the ingredient of love. That we should wait until we get married and have our own family to judge them. He would tell us to back off and leave his wife alone.

Dad loved to work; he loved being active. It took every breath out of us to get him to retire when it was time for him to retire. When dad got older, I knew that I must take very good care of him as he took care of me when I was young. Dad rarely got sick. He was sick for barely six months before he passed on. During those months, I dropped everything and focused on him. I took him to every doctor's appointment. I stayed in the hospital with him during his hospitalizations. Dad was always scared of being left alone in the hospital, so I made sure to be with him.

Taking him to the doctor's office for his blood works were the fun part of caring for him. Dad never liked needles and would behave like a child whenever the nurse or the phlebotomist would come near him to insert a venous catheter or to draw blood for a test. I used up all my sick days at work and almost lost my job because I was frequently taking off from work to be with dad at the hospital or to his appointments. During this time, dad was always apologizing for bothering me. He never liked to be a burden to anyone all his life.

I told him that he was never a bother to me, and it would never be a bother to care for him.

During the last days of his life, he kept pouring blessings upon me and my siblings. During his burial, it was obvious how blessed I was to have him as a father. The number of people that came to his burial was proof of the kind of person he was. People from all walks of life. A lady came to me during my dad's burial and said to me, "you are so blessed to have a father like him."

When I asked her what she meant, she told me a long story of how her elder sister used to work with a woman who was always telling them about this man who was in the business of helping people. How the man would provide for the widows and give often to the less privileged. The sister came to the burial because she was a partaker of this man's kindness and when she saw her co-worker and asked her what she was doing there, she told her that the deceased was the man she had told them about. There were a lot of stories like that during his burial. People that we don't know and have not met, came to mourn with us.

We celebrated my dad's life that day and it gave us the closure that we needed. My prayer is that myself and my siblings would carry on this legacy and give to our community like my Dad did. I am truly thankful that I had the opportunity to take care of him the much I did; because now that he is gone, I still remember all his words of appreciation and prayers he said for me when I was taking care of him.

One of those days, he held my hands and

told me that my children would take care of me more than I did for him. I cried so hard because for some reason, I felt like he was going to die soon which eventually happened. But that day, I felt so loved by him and I counted it as a blessing. Taking care of my loving dad was and still is a huge blessing for me. And I'm a true believer of 'what goes around comes around'. I believe that my children will care for me the way that I cared for my Dad.

CHAPTER 6

Sandra's Account
Trying to Care for My Mother

My mother had three of us, myself, and my siblings, with three different men. My sister was the first, then my brother, then myself. I'm the last of three. We never knew who our fathers were; our mother would never discuss that with us. My sister is three years older than my brother, who is two years older than me. Sometimes I feel like my brother and I share the same father because we look so much alike, more than we do with my sister. So, I think that we look like our father, while my sister looks like our mother because she is a replica of my mother, except for being responsible. My sister was basically the sole provider for my brother and me until we got to the point where we could take care of ourselves. She started taking care of us when she was about 10 years old and continued throughout her teenage years. She made sure to get us up and ready for the school bus every day.

My mother, on the other hand, did not care;

I still cannot understand why she had us if she didn't want us. My mother had my sister when she was 16 years old, she was a junior in high school when she got pregnant. She had a boyfriend who was about the same age as her, who denied the pregnancy because he said that he never slept with my mother. Obviously, my mother was already pregnant before she started going out with this boy. According to the story I heard, my mother was hanging out with the wrong crowd and would skip school most of the times. The story was that she got pregnant by an older man who was supplying her with drugs that she was using. The older man was already married with children at the time; she could not put the pregnancy on him. She decided to ask this innocent shy boy at her high school out.

He agreed to go out with her. After two or three dates, her pregnancy started showing. Because she did not want to get the man in trouble with his family and the law, she insisted that it was the boy at school that got her pregnant. The boy's parents refused to accept that the pregnancy was their son's because on the occasions that they went out, either his mother or father usually would be around. They were never comfortable with her hanging around their son. They knew she was up to no good, but they tolerated her because of her mother and because she made their son happy.

So, when she came up with the pregnancy story, they knew that she was lying. They waited until she had my sister to do a DNA test which confirmed what everyone already knew. It got the boy popular in school which made him go deeper into depression because he got depressed when she tried to put the pregnancy on him. It took him many years to get off the shock and depression that he went through. I learned that my mother went and apologized to him and his parents, saying that she did not know what to do when she found out that she was pregnant and that she wanted her child to have a father and a good life.

After all these shameful events, my grandmother could not take it; she died of heartbreak when my mother was about 19 years old. So, she was left to care for herself and my sister, who was almost three years old. She could not keep a job; always getting in trouble at work and would go to work sometimes intoxicated. Of course, she did not have any kind of education other than high school which she did not finish because she dropped out when she got pregnant. She refused to get her GED so that she could better herself. She was evicted out of my grandmother's house because she couldn't pay any of the overdue bills.

By this time, she was already in the system collecting WIC (Women Infant and Children), which is a government-approved supplemental nutritional program for women, infants, and children. She applied and was approved for it when she was pregnant, and it continued through my sister's infancy to toddler years. The food and other things that she was getting from that program were what sustained her and my sister. It was supposed to last until my sister turned five, but she got pregnant with my brother before the program could end. When she was evicted from my grandmother's house, she went and applied for what is called the Section 8 housing project, which is a voucher program funded by the federal government to help very low-income families get decent housing.

My mother was so irresponsible with all the help that the government was giving her to the point of selling her food voucher to buy drugs because she was addicted. She was introduced to drugs by the older man who we believe was my sister's biological father but who denied any involvement with my mother. She took a break after she was pregnant with my sister because she thought that the shy boy was going to take responsibility for the pregnancy. After she had my sister, she gradually went back to it; by the time she was pregnant with my brother, she had become a full-time addict. It still marvels me till today how we did not end up in foster care. You would think that because of her addiction and lack of parental instinct, the government would have intervened on our behalf.

After she had my brother, it did not take her any time to get pregnant with me. My sister was already five years old when I was born; by then my mother was already deep into drugs. She would have other dealers come over to the house; she would ask my sister to take us to the room while they stayed in the living room and dealt.

By the time my sister was eight, she had already started taking care of my brother and me. Sometimes, she would sneak over to our neighbors to ask for food when our mother had used our food voucher for drugs. Surprisingly, these neighbors never called child protective services on our mother; instead, they turned a blind eye and helped us with food and other essentials whenever they saw that we were hungry and in need.

When my sister was about 12 years old, she was sexually abused and raped by one of the men associated with our mother. I was around 7 years old at the time, and I still vividly remember the pain my sister endured that fateful day. Despite knowing about the assault, our mother showed no concern as it was in exchange for drugs. Due to her physical maturity, my sister was a target for abuse from these men until she became pregnant at around 14, which temporarily halted the abuse.

Upon discovering my sister's pregnancy, our mother took matters into her own hands and performed an abortion at our home. I recall seeing my sister in pain and bleeding but being too young to understand the gravity of the situation. It wasn't until I reached my teenage years that I fully comprehended what had transpired that day.

During the times when our mother would

disappear for weeks on us, my sister held our household together. She began working at a nearby grocery store at the age of 15 to support my brother and me. Her boss was aware of our circumstances and often provided her with groceries to bring home. We transitioned from WIC vouchers to an EBT card, a government program aimed at assisting low-income families with nutritional needs.

As my sister navigated high school, she secured numerous academic scholarships and student loans that facilitated her journey through nursing school. She pursued a career as a Neonatal Intensive Care Unit (NICU) registered nurse, drawn to caring for vulnerable infants due to the trauma she experienced when our mother forcibly terminated her pregnancy. Her dedication to nursing was remarkable, considering her responsibilities of supporting our family while juggling work and school.

Upon entering college, my sister made the wise decision to move out of our home to avoid the distractions posed by our mother and her associates. She played a pivotal role in shaping our educational aspirations, motivating my brother to become an engineer and me to pursue a career as an accountant/financial analyst. Eventually, we all moved out, leaving our mother and her destructive habits behind.

Years later, I learned from a former neighbor that our mother's health was rapidly deteriorating, prompting me to visit her despite my sister's reluctance. She had severed ties with our mother after leaving home, unable to forgive her for the hardships she endured. Meanwhile, my sister had established a successful career at a prominent hospital, where she met and fell in love with a medical doctor.

Their relationship flourished, leading to plans of marriage, and starting a family. However, they discovered that my sister's past trauma prevented her from conceiving due to the consequences of the illegal abortion inflicted by our mother. Despite this revelation, her fiancé remained steadfast in their relationship and proposed adoption as a means to realize their shared dream of parenthood.

Concerned for our mother's well-being as her health declined, I offered her temporary shelter at my home. Recognizing her struggles with mental illness possibly stemming from a lifetime of drug use and traumatic experiences, I felt compelled to provide support amidst these difficult circumstances.

Instead of being happy and appreciative of my kind gesture, she was very disrespectful to me. She kept telling me that I would amount to nothing, that I should be more like my sister, that I should make myself attractive to be able to get a man. I completely ignored her insolences and kept caring for her until I could not take it anymore.

She kept wanting to see my sister and telling me that we both need a man in our lives. I told her that my sister already had a man and was about to wed. She became silent and started complaining that she could not believe that my sister would think about getting married without introducing her to the man that she planned to marry. She was delusional, apparently, she had forgotten how she treated us and how she did not want us, the trauma that she caused us.

I got so scared that none of my relationships worked because they all want children, but I do not want any children. I do not want to bring children into this world and have to treat them like my mother treated us. I am not saying that I would be like her, but you never know, she was my mother, so I might have that trait in me.

I couldn't stand her insults while she was staying with me, so I had to put her in a home. She did not like that because it made her lose all controls. I went to visit her often, my brother went every once in a while, to see her but my sister never did. Her fiancé went with me one of the days that I went to visit her to introduce himself and to see what kind of mother that she was. She would not talk to us because she had complained about the food they serve there and asked that I move her back to my house, but I told her that she would be better off in the nursing home since she would have constant help. The fact that she had become so fragile, weak, and sickly, except for her mouth; I could not take care of her at home. At this point, she needed 24-hour care.

A few months after she moved into the old people's home, she started to adapt and adjust. Then one day she fell at the nursing home and broke her hip which was all bone;

she never recovered from it. She was put in a wheelchair, and she had to go to several rehabs for physical therapy after surgery. Her surgery site got infected. It was just from one thing to another until one day she was taken to the hospital again and she couldn't make it. The doctor said that she died of sepsis.

Mother did not give anybody an opportunity to care for her. Her life was destroyed from when she was sixteen years old, and she did not gain her life back. I forgave her all she did to us and tried to give her an opportunity to repent from her wicked ways, but she already made up her mind that she was going to die broken. If I must be honest with you, it was a big burden caring for her the little time that I did. I know that this is not what you want to hear but I must be honest with myself and with you, I do not wish my mother on anyone, not even my worst enemy.

During her funeral, it was just me, my brother, my sister's fiance', and about three staff from the home where she lived. She did not have many friends except for her fellow addicts who deserted her when she could not deliver anymore.

CHAPTER 7

Helen and Nick's Account
How We Cared for Mom

"I don't know if I'm the right person that you should be asking this question because I did not take care of my mother before she passed away, my brother did. But I can tell you the little that I can remember about mom.

My parents got married at very young ages; my mother was 18 years old, which was about the normal marriage age for their generation, and my father was 20 years old. After they got married, they did not start a family right away; instead, they decided to build a business. Their business grew over the years, and other people were coming to partner with them, but they refused and decided that it would be a family business.

A few years after their business started growing, they had my older brother, then my second brother, and I was the last child. Each time that my mother got pregnant, my father would work harder, double how he would, to make sure to be with mother at least during the delivery and few weeks afterwards to help mother at home. They were so much in love with each other and would never hide anything from each other.

We never lacked anything growing up; we went to the best schools in our city. My parent's business became a household name; it expanded so much that the two of them could not run it. They decided to hire a lot of people to help them with the business. Some of these people were living with us. The house was getting too big for mother to maintain by herself, so she hired a bunch of help because she did not want to leave the business for my father to manage on his own. Because of the helpers and maids that we had, mother never let me do anything, she had them do it for me. My brothers called me spoiled, but I did not see myself as a spoiled child because we all get the same level of attention from our parents.

Being the only girl, my dad never treated me differently, but my mom felt like I was a treasure that needed to be displayed for everyone to see. She made it look like I was the best thing that had happened in her life. Both our parents were really cool and soft spoken; they would not yell at us or the people living with us for any reason. Some of the people who lived with us took advantage of their kind heart, but some remained loyal.

When my dad passed away, my mom almost died with him. She went into deep depression and started having health issues. The business almost crashed and died with him; but my elder brother stepped up and took over. We all knew that it was going to be his one day, since he's the first child, that forced mother to step down and watch him.

My dad's death shook and devastated the whole family; people thought that it would be the end of our family and business, but it did not kill us. My mother never forgave herself after my dad died because she felt like it was her fault that he died. Father went for a business trip in a different state, mom would usually go with him to some of these trips. One of my parent's employees could not make it to work that week because his pregnant wife had gone into early labor, he went with his wife to the hospital. Because of that mom stayed back. The day that my dad was supposed to come home, he finished his business earlier than usual and decided to change his flight to an earlier one. He never liked staying away from mother for a while; when he told her that he was changing his flight, she was excited and told him to hurry home. Despite the fact that they were married for so long, they never stopped loving each other. Whenever I looked at them, I always prayed and hoped that I would find a man who would love me the way that my father loved my mother and that I would reciprocate like mother did with my father.

My mother believed that my father was hurrying home to be with her and hurried to his early death. He was in his mid-fifties when he died. The flight he boarded developed some mechanical issues and crashed, so we were told. Every passenger on board that flight, crew included died. It was the worst day ever.

My mother and our driver were at the airport waiting for him when they heard the sad news. My mother passed out and was taken to a nearby hospital by the ambulance that our driver called after he tried to wake her up. It was double bad news for us because our mother, who could have been there for us, was admitted at the hospital.

We were so confused when the driver came home and told us what happened. We did not know if we should go to the hospital or go to the airport to get more information on where and how the crash happened.

My elder brother decided to go to the airport with another driver and sent my brother and me to go stay with our mother at the hospital. When it was confirmed that my father was among the passengers who died in that crash and his body was identified, we picked up his body and put it in the morgue while waiting for our mother to recover from the shock so that we could fix a date for his burial.

During his burial, my mother was put on heavy medication that helped her through that first week. After the burial, mother was never herself again. She started being overly forgetful and would talk to herself. She kept believing that our father would come home one day. Some nights, she would stay up waiting for him to return from the business trip that he went for. She would ask us if we had heard from our father, if he had communicated his return time with us.

It became so bad that my elder brother had

to take her to a psych hospital to get her checked out and treated. The treatment helped a little bit because she was aware that I was getting married but kept insisting that I should wait until my dad got back to walk me down the aisle. She refused to accept the fact that he was dead. My mother's mental and medical conditions started affecting everything, our lives, the business, and her own life as well. We started losing our staff and our household helps.

My brother was trying his best to keep the business from going bankrupt and the entire household from crumbling down, that he paid less attention to his wife and children; it almost cost him his marriage. He started withdrawing from the family but not the business, he would check on mother every once in a while.

My second brother Nick also has a wife, and they have their own house. He was working as a business consultant back then and did not involve himself with the affairs of the family business because he believed that it belonged to our older brother, being the first child/ son, and he assumed the head of the household when father died.

Before my father's death, my parents had already planned out our lives for us. They had like a list of potential suitors who they thought were eligible to marry me. After my dad passed away and our family business started going down, some of these eligible suitors started disappearing one after another. My husband was the only man standing. He did not care about what was going on with our family business; he decided to stick around. We got married a few months after my father's funeral and moved to a different state.

Moving to a different state made it hard for me to be able to see my mother all the time, although I called her all the time. A year and a half to two years into my marriage, I had our first child (a daughter), and I had my mother come to stay with us for some weeks. I was glad that she came but she was requiring so much attention and monitoring, it was very hard for me to be able to care for my newborn and care for her at the same time; so, she left earlier than she was supposed to.

When I was pregnant with my twins, I visited her often so that she would not have to come to my house after the babies were born because my husband requested that I should be the one visiting her and not her visiting us. I didn't like it initially but accepted it and became comfortable with the arrangement over time. My mother did not agree with the arrangement when I told her about it but had to also accept it as long as he would allow me and the children to come visit her.

I feel like the reason why my husband did that was because after my father's death and our family business almost crumbled, he was the one who helped my brother to revive the business by investing a large amount of money into our family's business. None of my brothers could challenge him because of this fact, though Nick would, every once in a while.

By the time I had my last baby after my twins, my mother's condition had worsened. Although her cognition was still intact, she suffered a massive stroke that left her paralyzed on the right side. It also affected her speech and made it difficult for her to swallow anything. It took her some time to swallow even the smallest pieces of ground food and liquids; she started pocketing her food in her mouth.

Caring for her became burdensome. The caregiver who was hired to help with her care left because of the level of care that she required. We went through about four caregivers within a space of one year, and she was constantly being hospitalized. My brothers wanted me to take on her care because I'm her only daughter, and women are expected to care for their aging parents. They also felt that I should assume her care because I was a housewife and did not have a job. However, I could not do it even if I wanted to because my husband had already made it clear that she should not come over to our house anymore. He was willing to pay for her care as long as she did not come to stay with us.

One time, she was taken to the hospital and diagnosed with aspiration pneumonia. After that hospitalization, my brother Nick decided to take her home with him and care for her. His wife objected initially because she knew the care would fall on her, but she ultimately honored her husband's decision. Nick took a break from work to care for our mother because our aunt (mother's younger sister), who is a medical doctor overseas, heard about our mother's condition and decided to intervene by sponsoring her care. She sent a lot of medical equipment that mother needed to keep her going. She even came to Nick's house to visit and educate him and his wife on how best to care for our mother.

I'll hand over to Nick to tell you how he felt about taking care of our mother.

Initially, I did not want to take our mother in and care for her. I would have preferred to contribute what I could towards her care, but I couldn't. As a middle child, growing up, I was the most ignored and the least cared for. When my parents had my older brother, they were overjoyed because God gave them an heir to their kingdom and a successor to their business empire. When they had me, it was okay, but they would have preferred a female child. I was never paid any attention; all the focus was on my brother. Then they had my sister, and all the attention shifted to her. I knew from a young age that I should fend for myself. The house helps would always feel sorry for me because I often felt and looked abandoned by my parents. They were so focused on the growth and expansion of their business that they neglected their children's growth and struggles. I went through a lot of life struggles when I was younger, but they did not even notice.

I was constantly trying to impress them and would get anxious when they did not acknowledge my hard work. I went through depression and anxiety, and they were not even aware of it.

When my dad passed away, I was deeply saddened because I did not want him to miss out on my success, and he would never get the chance to be proud of me. I agree that they provided us with every need, but it was not enough for me because I never had the opportunity to be loved like my siblings.

So, when mom first got sick, I felt like she should go to her beloved son and daughter to care for her. When her condition started getting worse and her beloved could not care for her, I started contributing towards the caregivers' salaries. When my Aunt wanted to visit my mother and she did not want to travel to the state where mother was and wanted me to bring her to my house so that it would be easy on her since she only had a few days to visit. I agreed and brought mom to my house; her condition brought tears to my eyes; she had the same look that I had when I was younger (abandoned).

When my aunt came to my house to see my mother, she cried as if mother was already dead. She kept begging my mother not to leave her by herself in this world, since their parents and their other siblings had already passed away and they were all that was left of their father's lineage. Throughout her stay, she cared for mother like none of us would have dreamed to. She recommended and ordered some equipment that would help with mother's care. She taught my wife and me how to feed mother so that she doesn't choke or aspirate on her food or drink.

After I brought mom to my house, I put all my feelings to the side and started caring for her. After my aunt left, I had to take a long break from work to take care of my mother. It was not easy at first, but I pushed through it. Her first few days at my house, she would have tears running down her cheeks all the time; I don't know if it was out of guilt, disappointment, shame, pity, or her present condition.

My wife and I followed all the instructions

that my aunt gave to us on how to care for mother. During this period, my elder brother never bothered to visit mom, he would call on the phone and ask me or my wife how she was doing. My sister would also visit every once in a while, since her rich husband told her that he did not want my mother coming to their house. I don't know why I took up her care; I guess that I was still trying to gain her love and affection, but it was very unfortunate because she did not have any more to give. Not because she was sick but because she had already given it to our father, my brother, my sister, and of course the family business. At a point, I stopped trying to be loved.

On the night prior to the day that mom passed away, I fed her dinner, she ate better than other days. She did not fight like she would when taking her medications. When my wife was done cleaning her up and she was ready to go to bed, I helped put her to bed. That night I was telling my wife how she ate well and did not struggle with her medications and how she held my hand with her left hand and was trying to say something to me but couldn't, so I thought that she was trying to tell me that she had enough of the food. My wife looked at me and said that she did the same to her while she was cleaning her up, but the difference was that she had tears in her eyes when she held my wife's hand.

I woke up in the middle of the night to go check on her and I found her struggling to breathe. We took her to the hospital, and she died later that day. I was not feeling blessed when we were taking care of her because of how she treated me when I was younger; but my wife and I were blessed after she passed away. We were married for five years, and we did not have any children, we tried everything to conceive but couldn't. A few weeks after my mother passed away, we found out that we were pregnant. Thinking back to the day before she died, I believe that she blessed us for being there for her when the ones she loved most or showed most love to deserted and basically abandoned her and couldn't care less about her well-being.

CHAPTER 8

Amanda's Account
Putting Up With Our Mother

I have three sisters and one brother. My parents had my two elder sisters, my brother, me, and my younger sister. My dad worked as an accountant for a constructing company while my mom had her own business. She had something like a boutique at a local market.

When my eldest sister got married, her husband introduced my mother into his kind of business which was importing of clothing from outside the country. My mother traveled a lot; she would go to places outside of our original country like Dubai to buy goods and supply it to retailers. Her business expanded so much that she would travel out more than eight times in a year. She started making so much money than our father that she started losing respect for him.

It did not take long for our father to realize that mother's targeted customers were young good-looking bachelors. My father refused to lose the trust he had in our mother even when people would come to him and tell him about our mother; he would always tell them to mind their families and businesses.

My mother gradually started being controlling; she would want to tell our father how to run the family, that caused a lot of fights and arguments between them. My father was always a peaceful man who would let you win at every argument. My mother thought that it was weakness on his part. The disrespect that my mother had for our father was so much that they only spoke to each other when it's necessary, they slept in separate rooms.

My mom went and came whenever she pleased, and father overlooked it. He took care of us as much as he could. Mom started buying us over with gifts and money but that did not change the love we had for or relationship we had with our father.

Things went from bad to worse when my other sister Emily started going out with this young ambitious man; little did she know that mom was his sugar mummy. Our mother started his business for him. When Emily found out the relationship between her boyfriend and our mother, she threatened to expose everything. She physically had a fight with mother because she was deeply in love with this man, and she believed that he felt the same way with her.

He actually told my sister Emily how he was struggling and how our mother came to his rescue but with the condition that he would be sleeping with her. He was desperate, so he accepted the offer but regretted it all after our mother became over-controlling, telling him what to do and when to do it, how to dress, how to behave; basically, living his live for him. When my sister met him, he did not know who my sister was.

He knew that our mother was married with children but did not know that we were grown, he thought that we were babies. He told my sister that when our mother found out that he had a girlfriend, she threatened his life and the life of his girlfriend. That was why right after they met, he stopped communicating with her for a while, then came back to her. Our mother gave him the condition that he would have to introduce them, and that she will assess and make sure that she is the best fit for him. He agreed and planned on the meeting day.

My sister had told our mom that she would go and meet with some friends, mother told her to be careful. When she was ready to go, our mother was nowhere to be found. She just let our dad know that she was going out with some friends.

Meanwhile, her boyfriend told her that he would like to introduce her to his Aunty who had been like a mother to him. She was a bit nervous because she did not know how that Aunty would see her, what she would think of her, if she would like her. When she got to her boyfriend's house, she said that she had the strangest feeling like something bad was about to happen to her.

She was hugged and greeted by her boyfriend who went and got her some drinks. They sat there drinking and he was asking her what she would like to eat from a list of options that he presented to her when his supposedly Aunty walked out of the bedroom into the living room, my sister said that she was shocked to her bones. She ran out of the house in tears and kept running until she got home; it took her more than an hour.

By the time she got home, our dear mother was already there; calm as if nothing had happened. I remember she asked me where my sister was when she arrived. I told her that she had gone to see her friend. As soon as Emily got home, she ran straight to her room. I followed her because I noticed she was crying, but I couldn't enter the room as she had locked the door. I sat by her door, waiting for her dramatics to subside and for her to open up. As I sat waiting for her to share details about her meeting with her boyfriend's aunt, our mother knocked on the door, pleading with Emily to let her in before resorting to force. Emily finally opened the door and walked towards the living room. Our mother asked her to stop and talk, but she kept walking. Mother followed her, attempting to hold her arm to halt her progress. In response, Emily turned around, yelling, and pushing our mother, causing her to fall onto the couch. I stood there, watching like a spectator in a movie, as my sister behaved erratically, seeming possessed by a different entity.

I walked outside with Emily, who was now less hysterical and somewhat calmer. I queried her about what had overcome her, and she divulged everything that had transpired. Her revelations altered my perception and attitude towards our mother. While I strived to keep these feelings private, as I still resided under her roof, the experience prepared me for my future. I was unaware that our mother was involved with our oldest sister's husband, Rita. This newfound knowledge shed light on mother's frequent visits during Rita's early marriage. Mother claimed she was helping them, aiding in business training with Rita's husband. This association led to joint travels. I recalled an incident where Rita tearfully confided in our father while mother was away. Upon mother's return, tensions escalated as she vehemently defended herself against father's inquiries.

Emily reconciled with her boyfriend, who later repaid mother's investments in his business. Despite this, Emily severed ties with our mother, though she maintained respect. Following her marriage to him, they prohibited mother from visiting their home or business premises. When they had their first child, our eldest sister assisted them, further isolating mother. Laura, my other sister, married early due to mother's influence, adhering to her wishes out of a desire to please. Unlike Laura, I resisted such control, leading to strained relations and exclusion from mother's favors. It was our father who supported my education and shaped who I am today. I refrained from seeking assistance or guidance from mother, maintaining independence.

As for our brother Mike, he remained devoted to mother, blinded to her flaws. Despite attempts to highlight her misdeeds, he staunchly advocated unwavering love for parents. I met my husband during college, and after years of courtship, we wed once settled in our careers. When he expressed a desire to meet my parents, I scheduled a visit ensuring mother's absence. My father approved, offering blessings, while I disclosed some family history to my disconcerted husband. A disagreement ensued as he questioned my mistrust, citing mother's history with her sons-in-law. The conflict ended unfavorably, despite my attempts to convey mother's deceitful patterns, especially concerning Laura's husband.

A few years after I had my third child, our father fell ill and was abandoned by our mother, which was not surprising to us or to him. I had to take my dad in so that it would be easier for me to care for him. My other siblings chimed in during his worst times. Before he passed away, he begged all of us to forgive our mother so that we would be able to move forward with our lives.

Our mother only came a few times to see our sick father because he would not let her stay longer than usual. When father passed away, the daughters in our community made life a living hell for her. They put her through all sorts of punishment and extended her mourning period. They were very angry because they knew that she never treated our father well and our father refused for them to get involved when he was alive.

I felt blessed caring for my father, but I don't know if I would say the same about my mother. She did not like me as much as she liked my other siblings because we were always fighting silent battles. After father's death, and mother was done with the mourning and punishment imposed on her by the daughters, her business started going down. She lost all her business contracts. It was like our father took mother's business to the grave with him; and because mother had broken so many bridges, it was hard for her to bounce back.

Again, age was not on her side anymore and her beauty and charm were fading away, she could not attract and trap any more youngsters. A few years after father passed away, she started getting sickly and because she was banned from going to almost all her daughters' houses, my brother's wife would not let her into their home because she did not want to associate with her kind.

We did not abandon her, but she is not getting the kind of love that a mother would get from her children when they get old and frail. We are paying the help who is staying with her, and we take turns to go and see her. She is telling everyone who cared to listen to her that she has repented and made peace with God and her dead husband but did not see why her children are treating her like she committed the worst sin that cannot be forgiven.

She is saying all these because one of the times that I went to visit her, I told her that she needs to make peace with herself, her God, and her dead husband. I don't think that it would be a blessing taking care of my mother, but I won't say that it would be a burden since I already know that I'm obligated to take care of her because she is my mother. And I think that my siblings feel the same way. I in particular have been trying to find a way to forgive her completely but each time I remember what our father went through in her hands, it makes it hard for me. I have been constantly praying that God will grant me the grace to be able to forgive her and put all that in the past.

CHAPTER 9

Charles' Account
Being There for My Dad

I was born into an average family of six children, the first son with one elder sister, two younger brothers, and two younger sisters. From a young age, I already knew that it would be my responsibility to take care of my family. It is part of our culture that men should provide for the family and the first sons usually would take over those responsibilities from their fathers even after they have their own families. I grew up in a rural area with both parents working hard to provide for the family. My father worked with the country's coal cooperation; my mother was into trading.

She went into trading because it would be easier for her to take care of the family and still do her buying and selling. She would go to wholesale stores and buy some goods and sell them at retail prices. She would usually do this during school hours when we were all at school. By the time that we were home from school, she was already home and had food ready for us. Some days she would leave early in the morning before we woke up to buy the goods, and by the time we woke up to get ready for school, she would be home with breakfast waiting for us. She was a very hard-working woman.

The more I looked at her diligence towards our family, the more I wanted to grow up fast to be able to help her. My father, on the other hand, was also working hard, but because he had a steady job and income, his schedule was outlined, making it appear like he was not working as hard as my mother. They both had to keep up with these work and business arrangements because there were six of us plus the both of them; it was a full house. We were a very happy family and the envy of people around us.

When I was in middle school, I started helping by waking up very early in the morning to go with my mother to the early morning markets where she would buy stuff on wholesale; I would also help her after school with the domestic work. By the time I was in high school, I already had my own small business that I conducted before and after school. I also had a relative who had a construction company who would let me work with them during the weekends; this is how I was able to open my own construction business after college. I observed this relative of mine and his workers as they went about their business.

I did not have to take extra classes after college to open my own company. I did all these, and the money that I was making was going towards helping the family. Throughout my college years, I told my parents not to bother with my tuition but to concentrate on my other siblings' tuition which I also helped with. I was proud of my achievements and kept striving to do more.

I studied Business Administration in college. After graduation, I got a job with a local company in my city. The pay was decent but not enough for me to take care of my family the way I would like to. I started mapping out strategies on how to start my own business. Within two years of working with this establishment, I was able to save up some money and borrow some from our local bank to start my own construction company. It was not easy at first, but it got better afterward.

As soon as my business was well established,

I asked my parents to retire, and I placed them on monthly salaries. I was doing so well in this business that within a few years, I had branches where we were offering other services besides construction. We started home decorations and landscaping businesses. My siblings were all well taken care of. I waited for my elder sister to get married before getting married myself. When my elder sister got married, due to the wealth I had acquired, I asked her husband not to pay the dowry.

In our culture, the groom pays a bride price (dowry), but I requested him not to. After my sister got married, I helped establish her husband. Then after ensuring that my other siblings were doing well, I proposed to my girlfriend, who was in the healthcare industry. We got married and were blessed with three children (two girls and a boy). A few years later, my wife was invited to travel abroad for work. Initially, I did not want it because I felt like it would divide our family.

It was supposed to be a two to five-year contract. I expressed my concerns to her; she took my concerns to her contact, and they decided that they would sponsor the entire family. In our first year abroad, I ran my company from outside the country. It became exhausting, and in the second year, I traveled to train one of my younger brothers on how to run the business. I let my younger brother take over the business. I decided to open the same type of company in the state where I was living at the time.

It was not an easy task, but with the help of God and all the people He put in my life, I was able to establish a construction company. I went through school and got all the certifications that I needed. Never easy, I promise you.

The reason why I'm talking about my business instead of answering your question about whether it's a blessing or a burden to care for my parent is because they are related. While I was trying to get myself established in a foreign land and to get my family stabilized, I never stopped giving my parents their monthly allowances; even when I was struggling.

My wife has been used to me not asking her how much she makes, rather I would give her upkeep money; so, while we were in a foreign land, she wanted it to continue like that. It was very hard to keep up until I was approved for some loans which I used to start a new construction company. My company was doing well and in good standing, I was gradually paying back my loan.

One day the state where we were living decided to pass an immigration bill that affected my company. Despite the fact that the people I hired to work for me were legal and had proper documentation to that effect, they had family members that the new bill that was passed by the state affected. So, because of this new bill, I started losing my staff gradually. Within a space of one month, I lost almost all my staff; that caused a major setback for my company. It almost destroyed my family.

I couldn't afford my parents' monthly allowances anymore nor my wife's upkeep allowance; they were all expecting it from me even after I explained to them that I couldn't afford it anymore. So, it was now up to my younger brother who took over my company to take care of my parents. The first thing he did was get married with the little profit that he was making from the company and did not think to retain the company's good standing. I was paying the company's debts from the money that I was making from my new company.

He would deny ever having enough for his new family, let alone sparing any change for our parents. My parents started giving me so much pressure that I almost fell into depression. They would not ask my brother for any type of monetary help but would expect that I would provide every of their needs. I struggled for months, almost a whole year without any income, I started using my other skills to provide for my family.

My wife suggested that I go and take classes to help me with getting a certification on becoming a Certified Nurse Assistant (CNA). I did that, and I started working as a CNA at the hospital where my wife was working. It was not what I would like to do but I needed it. Due to the pressure that my entire family was putting on me, I had to cut my family off. I stopped communicating with every member of my household (my parents, and siblings).

They made several attempts to get me to continue to communicate with them, but I declined because it was causing me more trauma than not communicating with them. It was the hardest decision that I ever made judging by the fact that I've always been there for them. My wife stepped up and started helping in providing for the family after she saw how deep that I was going into depression. It was not easy for me because I grew up with the notion that it is the responsibility of the man especially the first son to take care of his family. I was ashamed of myself for not being able to provide for my family; it made me feel less than a man. I started losing my self-confidence and I became a little insecure; thinking that my wife would leave me.

After one year of struggle, I bounced back to my previous status. We had to move out of the state where they would not let the immigrants work or move freely to a different state and I was able to reinstate my company. Other than my wife and children, the rest of my family members did not know that my economic situation changed again for good. I maintained my decision on not communicating with my family members.

A few years later, I got horrible news that my father had suffered a massive stroke. As soon as I heard that news, I could not continue with my non-communication decision. I felt so bad; I felt guilty like I was the cause of his stroke. I had to travel home to go be with him. He was very lucky; he did not get any deficit with the stroke. Within a few months of treatment and physical therapy, he was able to regain his health. With that said, I was able to make peace with my parents. We went back to the way we were before my business downfall.

After I made peace with my family, everything about me changed. My business went from better to best, my marriage was restored, and I progressed more than I have ever done previously. It came to my understanding that the reason why the business that I left for my younger brother failed was because he was scammed. He got himself involved with scammers who promised him that they would supply him goods from Turkey, Dubai, and China. They sent him some few fake goods that got him involved with the law, so he had to shut the business down, but nobody cared to explain that to me. Because he thought that the business would make him richer than I left him, he decided that he would not let me know about it. If I had known about the business, I would have advised him against it, and he have been in this deep problem that he is in. I forgave him and tried to help him as much as I could because he learnt his lessons.

My parents were so happy to see the family coming back together as we used to be. It was a blessing to be there for him during the period of his stroke crisis and to put aside all our differences and grudges against each other. We have always kept in touch since then until now.

CHAPTER 10

Irene's Account
My Mother Caring for My Grandmother

Growing up, I have always noticed these brawls between my mother and my grandmother. I never understood what could be so bad that they would constantly be fighting with each other. Each time my grandmother came to visit or for medical check-ups, which were the main reasons for her visits, they would always argue about the tiniest things. My siblings and I would talk about it to try to figure out what the problem was. My mother would not talk about it, but you could tell that whatever it was, it had really hurt her and was still hurting her. Our father died prematurely at a very young age, but before his death, he tried so many times to reconcile the problem between my grandmother and my mother.

I remember my father saying to my mother that he did not understand what the problem was because none of their stories were making sense. My grandfather observed the strained relationship between mother and daughter with a heavy heart. He tried so hard to bridge the gap, to mend the wounds, but my grandmother's resentment had taken deep roots. My grandfather would often share stories of powerful women who had shaped the world, hoping to inspire my mother and grandmother and to counterbalance the negativity surrounding them. It was not until recently that my mother opened up to me about the problem they had because she was still hurt and upset with her even after her death.

She told me that her life was not like the fairy tales she often heard from the elders of the village or from the other girls her age. Instead of love and warmth from her mother (my grandmother), her life was shrouded in a dark cloud of bitterness. According to my mother, from the day she was born, her mother harbored an intense resentment towards her. My grandmother had dreamt of raising a strong and capable son who would carry on the family name and legacy. When she discovered she had a daughter instead, disappointment twisted into resentment, and she couldn't bring herself to embrace the child she held in her arms.

As the years passed, my mother grew into a bright and resilient young woman despite the constant coldness she faced at home. My grandmother would often compare her to the imaginary son she wished she had, making her feel inadequate and unloved. My mother thought that things would get better after my grandmother had my Aunties and my Uncles, but it got worse. She couldn't care less about her, and it was obvious. Just the mere fact that her mates were having boys as their first child and she was told that she would have a boy when she was pregnant, and she ended up having a girl, which destroyed her dream of measuring up with her mates caused so much resentment that lasted a lifetime.

My mother said that she grew up grappling with the scars of her past that persisted to the future creating an emotional distance between my mother and my grandmother, a chasm that seemed impossible to bridge. My mother's resentment simmered beneath the surface, a silent rebellion against the unattainable expectations that had haunted her since childhood. When my mother was of age to get married, my grandmother never cared who she married, and that hurt my mother so much because other young girls her age who got married around the same time had their mothers were helping them with their wedding planning. This actually made my mother's resentment of my grandmother worst.

In my culture, when a woman delivers a child, whether married or unmarried, her mother or grandmother will go and stay with them for a period to help with the newborn and give the mother some time to rest. When my mother had my elder sister, my father went and asked my grandmother to come and stay with them, she hesitated according to my mother. She did not want to come but because my father asked and because a lot of people in the community had started talking about the feud between my mother and my grandmother, she decided that she would go and stay with my parents.

As we grew older, I remember how my grandmother would always visit us whenever she had a doctor's appointment. Her presence often brought tension into the house. We hoped and prayed for her quick recovery so she could return home. When her health declined, she came to live with us. Although my mother took care of her, it was clear that caring for grandmother was a significant challenge for her. She felt obliged to care for her as the eldest daughter in the family.

When grandmother became very ill, my mother reluctantly continued to care for her at home because grandmother refused to go to any of her siblings' homes, claiming they couldn't provide proper care. She often blamed our mother for her siblings' failures. My mother's frustration didn't stem from a lack of love from grandmother or mistreatment in her childhood, but from the lack of love reciprocation when grandmother was in need and unable to show affection. We couldn't help our mother because we didn't know how, and we didn't want to upset grandmother or start conflicts like the ones in our past.

As grandmother's health worsened, she was hospitalized. Mother tried to get her siblings to visit before she passed away, but only one uncle came. He was always supportive of our mother whenever grandmother mistreated her. He was by my mother's side at the hospital when grandmother passed away. He then informed the other siblings of her passing and the need to plan her burial.

They seemed indifferent, asking for cost estimates to split the expenses evenly among them. During the funeral, it appeared that the planning and arrangements were left to my mother, who did her best to give grandmother a dignified farewell.

Before grandmother was laid to rest, my mother approached her and forgave her for everything, marking the second time she had done so. She recounted holding grandmother's hand in the hospital, asking for forgiveness for any wrongs she may have done. She let her know she had already forgiven her.

Considering the tumultuous relationship between my mother and grandmother, marred by conflicts and battles, caring for grandmother was likely more burdensome than a blessing, despite my mother never admitting it. Our bond with our mother is unbreakable. Despite once wishing not to have children due to fear of the repercussions of their conflict, upon meeting our father, she prayed for many children to demonstrate how to properly care for them. And she did an excellent job raising all of us.

CHAPTER 11

Meredith's Account
Living with Mum

I am Meredith. I have two sisters and one brother. Let me start by telling you how my mother got to where she is today or what happened that made her how she is.

Our father left our mother when we were very young, and that pushed her into drinking, trying to drink her heartbreak and sorrow away. She basically became an alcoholic. Many times, she would pass out on the couch, unaware of her surroundings.

One fateful day, when we were much younger, my younger sister was at home with our mother. She was still too young for school, while my other siblings and I were at school. Unaware that our mother was drunk, my little sister, hungry and in need of food, told mother that she was hungry. Mother asked her to bring out some food from the refrigerator. The poor little girl retrieved a leftover hamburger and tried unsuccessfully to wake our mother. Eventually, she took matters into her own hands.

At four years old, she fetched a stool, climbed onto it, and put the food in the microwave. Unaware of the little bit of aluminum foil in the burger wrap, she pressed the start button. A sparkly noise followed, then a loud bang. She fell off the stool, wailing. The noise, the smoke detector alarm, and her cries woke our mother, who found the house filled with smoke.

As our mother opened windows and doors to let the smoke out, the microwave was almost on fire, the house nearly burnt down, and the hungry girl remained unfed. All my mother could do was yell at her for trying to fend for herself.

Growing up into young adults, our mother continued her alcoholic lifestyle, leading to job losses. Despite this, she showed no signs of change. Witnessing her sadness and despair after our father left, I made a decision not to go through the same with men. I initially thought I was a lesbian but now realize I am bisexual, with a stronger preference for women.

I've had several female partners, in high school and beyond. I eventually dropped out of college due to personal challenges. While out with friends one weekend, I met a guy who showed interest in me. Surprisingly, we hit it off, leading to unexpected dating. I never anticipated someone like him asking me out.

We dated for several months, and he broke up with me. What happened was that after about seven months of dating, I realized that I was late with my monthly period. I checked back to see the last time that I had it and it was almost two months. As soon as I told him that I was late with my period, his attitude changed towards me; he would not answer my calls or respond to my messages.

I went and got tested and by then I was about 12 weeks pregnant. I kept trying to reach out to him, but he did not want to see me. I was so upset. I was starting to show, and he still did not want to talk to me, so I decided to pay him a visit. I got to his residence and knocked at the door; I knew that he was inside because I knew his schedule. I stood by the door yelling at him because I knew that he could hear me.

He just spoke to me through the door and asked that I leave his property. I kept trying to talk to him to reason with me, but he seemed not to care about me or my pregnancy. He straight out told me that he was not the father of my unborn baby. He stated that he knew that I was sleeping around. I told him that I slept around with women and not men; he was the only man that I was with. He refused to listen to me or to even open the door.

My anger overcrowded my judgement; so, I decided that it would be a great idea to kick down his door. I started kicking at his door until I heard the police siren approaching. He had called the cops on me like he threatened that he was going to do. The police officer who responded to the call asked me what the problem was and why I was kicking the door down. I started crying and told him my story. He went inside and asked him what was going on. Meanwhile, I was in handcuffs.

Initially, he told the officer that he did not know who I was. He stated that he had a girlfriend whom he already proposed to and was planning to marry. He later said that he knew me from college and that we hung out once or twice and that was it. Guess what? I was booked for trespassing, aggressive assault and harassment. I was four months pregnant and was in jail for one week. My mother claimed that she did not have the money to bail me out, that she had to borrow money from people; money that I would have to pay back to those people. I agreed to pay her back.

Meanwhile, in the midst of all these, I lost my job because I was locked up and I forgot to call them, so they fired me on the grounds of 'no call, no show.' After I was bailed out from the jail, it became really hard for me to find another job. I was pregnant, living with my mother and siblings. Oh, I forgot to tell you that as soon as I got pregnant, my sisters became evil. They would connive and turn our mother against me. I became a stranger in the house that I grew up in.

After few weeks that I got back to the house from jail, mother started asking for the money that she paid when she bailed me out; I was not working and did not have the money to pay her back. Our house became like a living hell for me. Every little thing that I do, I would always get in trouble. One day, momma got back from work and was super upset because my sisters told her that I ordered food and did not ask if they wanted any. I was pregnant and had hormonal changes that would make me crave certain food and my mother and sister knew this.

Sometimes I don't crave what we have in the house, and that day was one of those days. When momma came to me with her questions, I tried to explain to her that I did not have enough money to order food for everyone. She said that I shouldn't have bought food for myself if I was not ready to buy for others. We had a little exchange of words that escalated to physical fight. She slapped me and I was trying to stop her; she thought that I was trying to fight back and one of my sisters called the cops.

When they arrived, my mother told them that she got back from work, and I started fighting her and that she would like to press charges against me. Because of my record, they took me to the station, and I spent some days there.

After a few days, she came and got me released. When I got back home, I tried to be on my best behavior. I managed to put up with them until I had my son. After I had my son, I got hired. As soon as I got my first paycheck, I left the house. I got an apartment that I was sharing with my friend. Because I was finding it difficult to care for my son and keep up with my job, I asked if Momma would be able to babysit for me. She accepted because she had so much love for my son. She helped me for several months. I thought that she was sober until one day she was driving under the influence with my son in the car with her. I was so livid because I felt like she still has so much hatred for me to the point that she wanted to take one thing in my life that I love so much and that is stable. I took my son from her and promised her that she would never see my son again. From that day on, I distanced myself from my mother and my siblings. The reason I did this was that it was not the first time that she would do things to jeopardize my son's life. Sometimes my siblings would be there and do nothing.

I walked in one day to pick up my son. I did not find him where he would usually be, and as I was not on speaking terms with my sisters, I went looking for him. I could not find Momma either. I kept going around the house calling out for my mother, she never answered. Then I heard my son babbling in the bathroom. I went into the bathroom and found Momma passed out with my son in the bathtub. I tried to wake her up, but she was completely out. I left her alone because that was not the first time. I took my son, who was already shivering from sitting in the tub for a long time. I dried him up with a towel and wrapped him up to warm him up. Instead of leaving like I usually did, I decided to wait for her to wake up. It took hours before she eventually got out of the bathroom. I questioned her about what happened, and she either did not know what she did, or she knew but was pretending not to.

Another incident was when I came to get my son and found him playing by himself while Momma was passed out on the couch, with nobody else in the house. I did not even bother to wake her up; I just took my son and went home. All these incidents were why I banned Momma from taking care of my son. After the DUI incident, and seeing how my sisters behaved, I decided that I will keep to myself and take care of my son. I receive messages from my siblings that Momma has been trying to clean up her act for my son, but it doesn't change how I already feel about her. I have cared for her while I was

living with her, and I can assure you it was
never a blessing, as far as I'm concerned. I
will not put in the effort when she gets older
because she has my other siblings to care for
her.

CHAPTER 12

Angel's Account
Taking Care of My Parents

My parents got married early in their lives, and my sisters and I grew up as a family of four girls. Before my mother had me, our father had already been threatening to divorce her if she couldn't give him a male child. During her pregnancy with me, she was consumed with anxiety over this threat, leading to a lot of health issues that caused her to go into early labor. She fervently prayed for a son, fearing our father's rejection if she had another daughter. When I was born, she felt a twinge of disappointment but that didn't lessen her love for me compared to my sisters.

Upon hearing of my birth, our father cruelly sent a message to the hospital telling my mother not to return, as he had found another woman who had borne him the desired male heir. He made it clear that he no longer wanted her in his life. By the time my mother returned from the hospital, she found all her belongings strewn outside, the other woman already established in the house as his new partner.

Despite her pleas, our father remained adamant, blaming my mother for not providing a male child. He failed to grasp that the sex of a child is mainly determined by the male's contribution. Ignoring her sacrifices and efforts, he accused her of intentionally birthing daughters. Disregarding the pleas of neighbors, he forced my mother to leave, taking my sisters and me to her parents' home. We stayed with them until she regained stability to care for us.

Over time, my mother regained her strength, securing a job that sustained us. She worked tirelessly, ensuring we lacked for nothing within her means, never allowing us to suffer more than our peers in the neighborhood. Meanwhile, our father moved on with the other woman who bore him a son, creating the family he desired so much. We had little interest in their lives, as his neglect had left us detached.

Eventually, my mother seized an opportunity to bring my sisters and me to the United

States, where we each built our own families. Years later, a tragedy befell our father: his wife and children perished in a car accident, leaving him embittered despite their marital issues. It surfaced that the son she brought into their marriage wasn't his biological child. She had misled him, seeking a commitment he didn't want, and when she became pregnant by another man, she pinned it on our father to avoid single motherhood.

They lived great and happy lives from what I was told. The other woman would purposely go to places where she knew that our mother would be, just to rub it in her face that she had taken over her man and home. I heard that my grandmother would usually go to our father's place to ask him why he would treat our mother the way he did but would always get the same answer indicating that our mother disobeyed him and kept having female children. My grandmother would try to explain to him that it was God who gave them the children and that it had nothing to do with our mother disobeying him. At a point, he would send his newly acquired wife to get rid of my grandmother.

When my grandmother died, people wagged their tongues, saying that she died from a broken heart because she loved our father so much, being her first son-in-law. When we moved to the US, she was against it because she wanted our mother to stay and fight for what belonged to her. Our mother tried her best to fix her marriage, but our father was adamant about marrying the other woman with a son.

When we first came to America, things were really tough for us. We lived with one of my mother's cousins who had been living here for a while. He helped my mother get a job, and he and his family helped take care of us. Since we all completed our high school before coming to the States, it was easy for my elder sisters to get jobs and start helping. They worked through college, graduated, got good jobs, and got married. I was the last one to marry.

After we all got married, our mother decided to go back home to be with relatives she left when we migrated to the States. She lived there and would often visit us and get her health checked. After a few years of back-and-forth visits, we decided it would be best for her to live here. It was agreed she would live with me since I was widowed and had very young children; it was best so she could help with my children. She goes back home every once in a while, and also visits my sisters.

After the tragic incident with my father's other family, he started reaching out to us. Our mother forgave him but vowed not to have anything to do with him again. My sisters refused to forgive him and didn't want anything to do with him. He came asking for forgiveness because when his other family died in a crash, people started saying it was karma taking his family due to how he treated our mother. I'm not sure if he came back to apologize because of his family tragedy or if he was truly sorry for abandoning us. Whatever his reasons were, our mother and I forgave him.

As years went by, my sisters started tolerating him; they would talk to him with reservations. He comes to the United States to visit but prefers to live at home. He visited the US until he started having health issues, so he stopped coming. Meanwhile, our mother, who was living with me, got sick. Her health deteriorated, along with her memory. She started getting confused, not following instructions anymore. I had to quit my job to stay at home and care for her.

We tried putting her in a memory care home once, but she cried so hard when she learned of our plans. She did not last a month there; she fell and broke her hips. After a few months in the hospital, when she was discharged, I decided to take her home with me. I tried hiring a caregiver, but she would not listen to the caregiver. Instead of paying the caregiver to watch her while doing the work myself, I decided to resign from my job to care for her full-time.

It has not been easy taking care of her, but when I remember what she went through and what she endured because of us, I care for her with joy and happiness in my soul. Caring for her has been very challenging and demanding, but I thank God for the strength that He has bestowed on me.

Sometimes, she would get so confused and combative with me. However, when she calms down, she starts apologizing to me for how she treated me. I don't hold any of these things against her because she is ill and is not always aware of what's going on around her.

One day, I woke her up in the morning to give her a bath, and she became angry with me, accidentally punching me. I reassured her that I was just trying to help, and she looked at me, tears in her eyes. I hugged her and reassured her that I understood.

She often becomes confused and angry because she doesn't understand why she should be confused and not remember the people around her. Meanwhile, while I was caring for my mother, our father fell ill and was admitted to a local hospital back home. Since he chose to live at home rather than in the States with the rest of us, we've been paying one of our cousins who lives back home to keep an eye on him.

I received a phone call from that cousin reporting that our father was having difficulty breathing, his stomach was distended, and he was taken to the hospital. The doctors discovered that he had an obstructed bowel and needed surgery. They requested money for the surgery, but I instructed them to wait until I arrived before proceeding. I arranged for emergency travel, with my sisters taking turns caring for our mother in my absence.

Upon arriving home, I found my father's condition very serious, and the doctors were urging immediate surgery. I consented to the surgery, and as they prepared to take him to the operating room, he called for me. With tears in his eyes, he asked for forgiveness for how he had treated us, especially me. He expressed regret for his past beliefs about the importance of having male children. He prayed for me and pleaded for my continued apologies to my sisters and mother on his behalf.

After the successful surgery and ensuring my father was safely back home, I returned to care for my mother. My sisters had stories to share about her. She had grown so accustomed to me that my absence made it challenging for them to care for her. Upon seeing me, she found peace within herself. I found myself shuttling between my parents, caring for both my mother and father. Though my sisters do assist at times with our mother's care, the responsibility weighs heavily on me. Despite the challenges, I find solace in fulfilling my duties.

CHAPTER 13

Ella's Account
Relearning to Care for My Mother

My parents had seven of us: four older brothers and two younger brothers. Being the only girl in the midst of six boys was not easy. You might think they would treat me like a queen or at least a princess, but no, they treated me like one of them, though they were over-protective of me. I started cooking for the whole family and any guests we had at the early age of about seven or eight. Boys are always hungry, and my brothers were no exception. My mother couldn't keep up with their appetites, so I stepped in to help.

I've always loved watching my mother cook ever since I was very young. She noticed my interest and started teaching me how to cook. I enjoyed helping out because she would lavish me with praise whenever I did something well, which motivated me to keep doing things that would earn me more compliments. Cooking wasn't the only thing I helped with; I also assisted in keeping the house clean and organized. I especially enjoyed accompanying my mother to the local market, where people often remarked on how much of my mother they saw in me. I've always been and still am my mother's carbon copy.

As I grew into a beautiful young lady, people began to expect a lot from me. They started asking my mother if suitors were coming to ask for my hand in marriage. Even after high school, I remained homely, continuing to assist my mother with household chores, as our culture dictated that such tasks were meant for women. One day, while on our usual trip to the local market, a flashy car drove past us and stopped. The person inside greeted us, and though I didn't recognize him, my mother remembered him from his childhood, as a close friend of my youngest uncle (my father's brother).

He visited us at home later, accompanied by my uncle, introducing himself as a childhood friend who had recently come to visit. Following that visit, my life changed as I eventually married my uncle's friend and moved to his location. My education was put on hold when I became pregnant with our first child right after the wedding, despite having been accepted into one of the best colleges in my area. I postponed my admission due to the pregnancy. After our second child was born, I decided to resume my academic pursuits.

My parents agreed to marry me off to the first suitor because they believed it would benefit the family by reducing the mouths to feed, and they hoped the in-law would support the family in any way possible. Living in a different country made it challenging to have my mother with me during my pregnancies and after childbirth. Several years after my second child's birth, I attempted to invite my parents over, but their visa applications were denied. I stayed in touch with my family, visiting whenever I had the chance. Over time, my brothers started their own families, moving to various countries, states, and cities.

My husband always went above and beyond to ensure the well-being and comfort of both my family and me. Without complaint, he would often send money and other forms of assistance to support my family, particularly my brothers who benefitted greatly from his kindness. As grateful as I was for his generosity, there came a point where I began to feel a sense of being taken advantage of. Despite my brothers being financially stable, they seemed to rely solely on me to address our family's financial needs.

In an effort to rebuild and renovate our family home, I undertook the task alone, receiving no acknowledgment for my efforts as it was viewed merely as my duty as the daughter. My husband and I worked tirelessly to provide for not only my immediate family but also our extended relatives. My father, on the other hand, consistently praised and encouraged me to continue helping those less fortunate or in need, always leading by example with his own altruistic actions.

Following our father's passing, the responsibility of overseeing the funeral arrangements fell upon me. Despite the challenges and my own obligations, I could not turn away from my family in their time of grief. With a heavy heart, I returned to my hometown to assist with preparations and bid a final farewell to our beloved father.

Throughout the process, my brothers and I set aside our differences, coming together to honor our father with dignity and respect. As we laid him to rest, surrounded by loved ones, a profound sense of closure washed over me, knowing that we would find strength in each other during this difficult time.

In the days that followed, I worked tirelessly alongside my brothers to ensure every detail was handled with care. My priority was to provide comfort to my grieving mother, offering her solace and support as we navigated through our shared sorrow. Despite the weight of our loss, we found solace in each other, drawing upon the bonds of love and kinship that united us.

After the burial, my efforts to bring my mother to live with me proved unsuccessful, partially due to her mourning process. Ultimately, she chose not to relocate and preferred that I visit her instead. Time passed, and circumstances evolved, leading her to decide she was content remaining where she was, as I continued to visit her regularly.

My mother missed out on all my children's milestones but was a part of my nieces' and nephews' milestones. I was constantly applying for a visa for her to come and live with me, but she kept getting denied of a visa. When my daughter got married and was getting ready for her wedding, she invited my mother herself just in case I was doing something wrong, but she was denied yet again.

My daughter just had a baby, which made my mother a great-grandmother, and my daughter started petitioning the visa process to see why my mother was being denied. My daughter wanted my mother to witness the birth of her first great-grandchild, but the visa agency deprived her of that privilege. After my daughter's petition, my mother was finally granted a visa.

A lot has changed in my mother, both physically and mentally; she is not as strong as she used to be, and her mind is not as sharp either. When she came over here, my daughter wanted her to go straight to her house, but I pleaded with her to let me care for her for at least a week before letting her go anywhere else.

Being that it had been a while since I'd been with my mother, there was a lot about her that I did not know, despite traveling almost every year to visit her. Most of the time that I went to visit her, it was hard to have alone time with her; other family members, both extended and immediate, would come around to spend time with us, depriving us of moments to be alone and have intimate conversation. Her visit became a relearning period for me.

Years of distance had created a significant void between my mother and me, and we struggled to find common ground. We felt like strangers trying to get to know each other and were super conscious of each other, trying not to do anything to irritate or upset the other. It was the strangest period ever; I did not realize there had been such a big gap between us, as we used to be inseparable when I was younger.

I had to take some time off from work to be able to reconnect with my mother. I started by learning her likes and dislikes, the type of food she enjoys, any medical conditions I was unaware of, her daily routine, strengths and weaknesses, and her expectations of me. Through laughter and tears, we shared hopes and fears, joys, and sorrows. We talked late into the night, reminiscing about days gone and dreaming of the future.

Slowly but surely, our relationship began to heal, strengthened by love and forgiveness. It was a memorable experience; I felt like a child again. We started catching up on things from the last time we were together, years of missed intimate conversations. There were things that had happened in my life that my mother did not know about and vice versa. Our first few days together were filled with emotions; we both had heart-breaking stories we never shared with anyone because we did not trust them with our secrets.

Although I initially asked my daughter for a week with my mother before she went to stay with her, she ended up spending more than a week with me as I couldn't bear to let her go. As the days turned into weeks, my mother's health improved, her spirits lifted by the love we shared.

After reconnecting with my mother, I felt truly blessed to have her back in my life. When she eventually went to my daughter's house to spend time with her, her husband, and my grandchild, I found it challenging to let her go. I felt like I had lost my mother, found her again, and was about to lose her once more, and I didn't want that to happen.

So, I constantly stopped by to check on them. We have decided for her to stay with us and not return to her town except for visits. I am super glad and excited to have my mother back in my life and my children's lives. It is an honor and a huge blessing to care for my mother.

CHAPTER 14

Nobel's Account
Caring for My Ailing Mother

I am the sixth son in a family of eight boys, born into a bustling household filled with laughter, love, and the occasional chaos that comes with a large family. From the moment I came into the world, I shared a special bond with my mother. My birth was marked by both joy and sorrow because my mother had several complications that almost took her life. Due to these complications, she was faced with the decision of who should live - her or me.

As the story goes, my mother chose to save my life; she insisted that if it came down to saving only one person, it should be me over her. When she was around 30 weeks pregnant with me, during one of her antenatal visits, an ultrasound revealed that the baby she was carrying was not moving. Subsequent tests confirmed the devastating news that the baby had no heartbeat. She was immediately rushed to the hospital for further evaluation and likely intervention.

Doctors determined that an emergency surgery was necessary to save my mother's life. Despite her disbelief that I was truly gone, she consented to the procedure. After the surgery, she asked to hold her lifeless child before the final goodbye. As she cradled me close to her heart, tears falling on my face, a miraculous turn of events unfolded. Remarkably, as her tears touched me, colors returned to my face, a pulse could be felt, and I began to breathe.

In that extraordinary moment, she held onto me tightly, feeling a surge of life within me. Even the nurse present was astonished by this sudden turn of events. From being declared stillborn to this miraculous revival, the unfolding of events was beyond comprehension to all involved.

This miraculous event led my mother to name me Miracle. It became a symbol of hope and faith for her, a reminder of the extraordinary circumstances of my birth. This title stayed with me through my adulthood, reminding her of the divine intervention she believed had occurred.

However, to everyone else, I was and will always be known as Noble.

Learning about the incredible circumstances of my birth deepened my bond with my mother. I made a promise to always be there for her, to provide care and companionship, and to ensure she never felt abandoned. This life-changing event also sparked a curiosity in me about faith and the divine. I began to question and research the existence of a higher power, grappling with the mysteries surrounding my own birth and survival.

Reflecting on the hospital records detailing my stillbirth and the subsequent revival, I came to realize the profound impact of this event not only on my life but also on the faith and belief systems that I held dear. The promise I made to my mother remained a guiding light in my life - a commitment to always be her Miracle, her source of strength and support, no matter what challenges lay ahead.

Years passed. I finished school, got a good job, found love, and married a woman I love and adore. We started a family of our own. Amidst the joy of building a life together, I never wavered in my dedication to my mother, especially after my father passed away. I made sure to visit her regularly, sharing stories of my growing family and seeking her wisdom in times of need.

My mother loved my wife and children with everything she had; she carried the love she had for me onto my family. Some may wonder about my brothers, questioning if she cared for them. The answer is yes. She loved and cared for all of us passionately but had a special bond with me. It used to bother my father and brothers, but they got used to it after a few years.

Before my father passed away, he would joke about me taking over his wife and say that I would have to give him back all that he spent on my mother since I've taken over his woman. It became a joke in the family where my brothers would call me a wife snatcher.

It took me a while to bring a lady home to my mother because I thought she would judge whoever I brought home, until I met my wife. My mother fell in love with her the moment she saw her. While I was relieved, my mother told me that it wouldn't have mattered to her who I went out with or married as long as we made each other happy and loved each other deeply, which was indeed the case with me and my wife.

We had several years of unconditional love; we went through trials but triumphed victoriously. Our marriage was blessed and fruitful, and my mother was a big part of that. She was with us in our good times and our bad times.

Life took an unexpected turn when my mother fell ill. As her condition worsened, we (my brothers and I) faced the difficult decision of whether to place her in a care home or have someone care for her, which was hard to find. For me, there was no question – I couldn't bear the thought of my mother spending her final days in a care facility.

With unwavering determination, I brought my mother into my own home, despite knowing the strain it would place on my already fragile relationship with my wife. Unfortunately, my wife's character and attitude started changing when my mother became ill and was unable to do the things she once could.

Unable to understand the depth of my bond with my mother, my wife grew resentful of the situation. Our once-happy home became fraught with tension as disagreements escalated, leading to my wife leaving the house and eventually filing for divorce.

Heartbroken but resolute, I chose to prioritize my promise to my mother over my marriage. I watched as my family fractured, but my devotion to my mother remained steadfast. I believe it when people say that your mother can jump in front of a gun for you or take a bullet for you, whereas your wife, partner, or anyone else might not. If my mother went through what she did to have me, I should be willing to go to the moon and back for her.
Years passed in a blur of caregiving duties, doctor's appointments, and bittersweet moments shared with my mother. Despite having five older brothers and two younger brothers, it seemed like I was our mother's only child. The bond we shared was so evident that I became the center of our mother's world, even before our father passed away. While our father couldn't believe that our mother poured all her love

on just one of her eight children, my brothers knew that the love she had for me was special.

My family thought that being so loved meant I wouldn't amount to anything and expected me to fail, but I proved them wrong. Despite the abundant love and care, I ensured I always did the right thing. I pursued education like my brothers, landed a good job, got married, and started my own family, just like each of them.

Then, the inevitable happened – my mother's health declined rapidly, and she was admitted to hospice care. It devastated me to witness my once vibrant mother fade. I spent every precious moment by her side, holding her hand, and expressing love and gratitude for all she had done for me. Memories of our cherished moments together would bring tears to my eyes when I was alone.

During her last days, weakened and struggling to breathe, my mother held my hand, looked into my eyes with tears, and called me her little miracle. She expressed that I was her greatest blessing and urged me to reconcile with my wife, asking for forgiveness for overshadowing her with attention. Her words moved me to tears; even in her final moments, all she cared about was my happiness and our family's unity. I promised to honor her wishes.

When she took her last breath, it felt like a piece of my heart had been ripped away. In the quiet aftermath, grief consumed me. I mourned not just the loss of my mother but also the shattered dreams and the toll her sickness took on my marriage. Despite the pain, there was solace in knowing I had kept my promise and that she departed feeling deeply loved.

It was a privilege to be cherished by my mother and a blessing to care for her in her final days. I had vowed not to let her be alone, and I am grateful to have fulfilled that promise. She always saw me as her little miracle, but she didn't realize she was my miracle too. Her tears and unconditional love revived me. From the start until her last breath, she never gave up on me. I loved her immensely and hoped to be mother and son again in our next lives.

CHAPTER 15

Mena's Account
My Mom and I

I am the first child in a family of four. I have two younger brothers and one younger sister. Growing up, I was a whirlwind of energy, an outgoing teen with a spark of rebellion in my family's otherwise orderly existence. From a young age, I danced to the beat of my own drum, always pushing against the boundaries set by my parents. Their rules felt like chains to my free spirit. I felt like I was in a cage, and I couldn't bear the thought of conforming to their expectations.

I was not rebellious initially, but my mother made me like that. I needed to buy a gift for my friend who was celebrating her birthday. My father wanted to give me the money, but my mother asked him not to because she did not like that friend of mine. So, she told my father that she asked me to do some chores and I refused. Because of that, my father withheld his money. That was not all; I was not allowed to attend the birthday celebration. I got to school the next day and was made fun of for not going to the celebration, which made me very furious.

Despite my parents' warnings and admonishments, I continued to live on the edge, chasing excitement and adventure wherever I could find it. I would skip school sometimes, stayed out late, and ran with a crowd that made my parents' hair stand on end. But try as they might, they couldn't tame my wild heart.

As the years went by and I grew older, my rebellious streak only intensified. Out of despair, my mother decided that enough was enough. She convinced my father to stop giving me my allowances, hoping that financial strain might finally break me and bring me to my senses. When I realized what had happened, I was very furious at my parents for making such a decision against me. Feeling betrayed and abandoned, I cut off all communication with my mother, ignoring her at home. This caused our relationship to strain to a breaking point as I stubbornly refused to listen to reason.

It was so bad that I would tell her about parents-teachers-organization (PTO) meetings at my school, and she would not attend. So, I devised a plan; I had a woman who had a store a street away from our street. I always go to her store to buy stuff. I went to her and asked if she could come to my school and represent my mother because my parents traveled and would not be able to attend the meeting. I convinced her that I would come to her store and help her as a way of appreciating her coming to my school in place of my mother.

The reason why I needed her to go to my school was that this was my last chance to take my parents to talk to my teachers; otherwise, I would be expelled from school. My parents did not know how I was able to stay in school; they knew that I was supposed to be expelled if they did not attend that meeting. They could not figure out what I did or how I pulled it, but they continued to pay my tuition until I graduated from school.

As years passed by, my life took unexpected twists and turns as the friends I once thought were my allies turned out to be more interested in chaos than camaraderie. Slowly,

I began to realize that the path I was on led nowhere but darkness. My eyes opened when I was introduced to this girl by her cousin who was my friend. This new friend was very beautiful, humble, and a very good girl. Whenever I went to visit her, as soon as it started getting dark, she would ask me to start leaving because it's not good for a young lady to stay out late.

The first time she came to my house, my parents were skeptical about her until they realized that she was a great person. My life changed after meeting her. She started making me see the goodness in people, especially my family members. This relationship with this girl turned my life around; it changed things at home for me, my parents changed their attitude towards me, and I became a different person at school, at home, and everywhere. With this newfound determination, I made the difficult decision to change my ways. I distanced myself from my old friends and sought out new, positive influences. It wasn't easy, but gradually, I started to rebuild my life on firmer ground.

As my transformation took root, I found myself reconnecting with my family. It wasn't easy at first, and there were many wounds to heal, but my parents welcomed me back with open arms. They had never stopped loving me, even when they disagreed with my choices. Together, we forged a new relationship, one built on understanding and forgiveness. My mother watched with pride as I blossomed into a confident, responsible young woman. And as for me, I realized that sometimes, the greatest rebellion of all is the courage to change for the better.

My transformation into a responsible young woman didn't just change my own life; it also brought me closer to my family. After a few years of the changes to my life, I fell in love and got married. After I got married, I was blessed with two children, and my family could not be any happier. My parents never believed that I would become who I have become. With this newfound maturity and compassion, I embraced my role as a supportive daughter, especially when my father fell ill.

When my father's health began to decline, I and my mother with my husband's support rallied together, providing round-the-clock care and comfort. We shared the burden, standing by each other's side through the toughest of times. My love for my parents only deepened as we faced adversity together. But fate can be cruel, and tragedy struck when my mother unexpectedly passed away while caring for my father. The loss shattered not just my world but my entire family.

I felt as though a part of my heart had been ripped away, leaving an unbearable emptiness in its wake. Devastated by grief, I struggled to come to terms with the sudden loss of my mother. I found solace in the memories we had shared, but the pain of her absence weighed heavily on my heart. Although that in the midst of my grief, I found a glimmer of hope in the love I had found and nurtured with my husband. He became my rock, offering unwavering support and understanding as I navigated the turbulent waters of loss and sorrow.

Together, we leaned on each other, finding comfort in our shared love, and forging a path forward, one step at a time. And though my mother's absence left a void that could never be filled, I carried her memory in my heart, finding strength in the legacy of love and resilience she had left behind. Despite my own sorrow, I remained steadfast in my commitment to caring for my father.

I drew strength from the love we shared as a family, determined to honor my mother's memory by continuing to be there for my father in his time of need. In spite of the pain of losing my mother and the challenges I had faced along the way; I had emerged stronger and more resilient than ever before. In the years following my mother's passing, I had continued to prioritize my family, cherishing every moment with my father, siblings, and husband. Together, we had weathered life's ups and downs, drawing closer together in the face of adversity.

But as time marched on, new opportunities began to beckon to me as I had always been ambitious, with dreams and aspirations that reached far beyond the confines of my past. And now, with the support of my loved ones behind me, I felt ready to pursue those dreams with renewed determination. Although I encountered some obstacles and setbacks along the way with moments of doubt and uncertainty that threatened to derail my progress; but each time, I drew strength from the lessons of my past, reminding myself of the resilience that had carried me through the darkest of times.

And as the years passed, my hard work and dedication began to pay off. But amidst the hustle and bustle of my busy life, I never forgot the values instilled in me by my parents—the importance of love, family, and staying true to oneself. No matter how far I strayed from the path, those guiding principles remained steadfast, grounding me in times of uncertainty and guiding me toward a brighter future.

And as I looked back on the journey that had brought me to this point, I couldn't help but feel a sense of gratitude for every twist and turn along the way. For it was those experiences, both joyful and painful, that had shaped me into the woman I had become—a woman unafraid to chase my dreams, no matter where they might lead.

A few years later, my father's health worsened, and he couldn't bear the ailment; he passed away. With his passing, I found myself once again plunged into the depths of grief. The loss weighed heavily on my shoulders, leaving me feeling writhing in sorrow. But amidst the pain, I knew that I had to be strong for my family, especially for my younger siblings who now looked up to me for guidance and support. As the eldest sibling, I took on the mantle of responsibility with a heavy heart.

I knew that I couldn't let my grief consume me, not when my family needed me the most. With unwavering determination, I set out to provide for my siblings, determined to honor my father's memory by keeping my family together. Despite the challenges that lay ahead, I refused to be daunted. I rolled up my sleeves and got to work, taking on whatever jobs I could find to make ends meet.

It wasn't easy, juggling the demands of work and caring for my siblings, but I refused to let them down. Through it all, I drew strength from the love and support of my husband, who stood by my side through thick and thin. Together, we formed a united front, facing each new challenge with courage and resilience.

As the years passed, my sacrifices began to bear fruit. With hard work and determination, I was able to provide a stable and loving home for my siblings, ensuring that they never wanted for anything. And though the road ahead was fraught with uncertainty, I faced it head-on, knowing that as long as we had each other, we could weather any storm.

In the midst of my grief, I found solace in the knowledge that I was carrying on my father's legacy, keeping our family together through the toughest of times. And though the pain of loss would always linger, I took comfort in the bonds of love that held us together, stronger than ever before. I am very happy and fulfilled that I was able to care for my parents; I am glad that I turned a new leaf and made them proud before they left this life.

I'm super happy that my life was changed before all these sorrowful events that befell my family. I am glad that my parents equipped me for this responsibility, and I'm happy that I did not let them down and will never let them down. I know that they would always watch over us from wherever they are. And my siblings grew into great and responsible adults; all thanks to the life that my parents instilled in all of us.

CHAPTER 16

Erika's Account
Living With and Caring for My
Racist Mother

I was a bright-eyed, freckle-faced Caucasian girl who grew up in a medium-class environment. My neighborhood was a melting pot of cultures, where people from different ethnicities lived side by side. From a young age, I found joy in the diversity of my community; I loved the vibrant colors of the Hispanic celebrations and the rhythmic beats of African drums during block parties. My neighbors became my extended family, and I cherished the friendships I formed with both black and Hispanic children in my neighborhood.

However, there was one person who didn't share my enthusiasm for my diverse group of friends: my mother, who held onto outdated prejudices and stereotypes, and she couldn't understand why I would want to spend time with children who didn't look like me. I would always get in trouble whenever I went out to play with the other children. My mother would call me every name in the book for liking people from a different culture than mine. But it didn't bother me; I remained steadfast in my belief that friendship knew no boundaries of race or ethnicity. I saw beyond the color of my friends' skin and embraced the richness of their cultures and experiences.

My relationships with my neighbors were actually me trying to prove to them that I was not like my mother; everyone in the neighborhood knew that my mother was a racist, she wasn't hiding her dislike for people from another ethnicity. Because of how my mother was with them, they thought that I was like her, but I don't have the same perception as my mother. Out of spite for my mother, I started going out with this African American boy. He was the most handsome and humble human that I ever saw.

Then the unexpected happened; my heart raced as I sat in my childhood bedroom, staring at the small plastic stick that held my fate in its hands. The pink plus sign seemed to mock me, confirming what I already knew deep down; I was pregnant with Malik's child. Tears welled in my eyes as I thought about how to break the news to my mother. I knew that it would not be easy, but I never anticipated the storm that would follow.

When I finally mustered the courage to tell my mother about the pregnancy, her reaction was beyond anything I had imagined. The air crackled with tension as my mother's face twisted with anger and disappointment. The first thing that came out of her mouth was, "You're pregnant? And with that boy?" My mother's voice was laced with disdain as she spit out the words. I felt a lump form in my throat as I tried to explain that Malik was a kind and loving partner, regardless of the color of his skin. But my mother's prejudice ran deep, and she refused to listen.

As the weeks passed, the rift between me and my mother widened into a gaping chasm as our relationship now resembled a battlefield, with harsh words and bitter arguments echoing through the walls of our home. I was torn between my love for Malik and our unborn child, and the acceptance of my mother. Despite the turmoil, I remained resolute in my decision to stand by Malik and our unborn child. I knew that our love was worth fighting for, even if it meant standing up to my own mother.

Another unexpected turn of events surfaced when I discovered that Malik had not notified his parents about our little gift because he did not know how. It happened that his parents had previously had issues with my mother that involved the police; my mother thought that they were immigrants seeking their permanent stay and reported them as illegal residents. It so happened that they were Americans but relocated from their home state to our state. That incident created a bad taste in his parents' mouths.

As the due date drew near, my heart grew heavy with the realization that neither my mother nor Malik's parents would be at the hospital to share in the joy of their grandchild's birth. But I refused to give up hope that someday, somehow, they might find a way back to each other. And when the day finally arrived, and I held my beautiful baby girl in my arms for the first time, I felt a rush of love and gratitude wash over me.

In that moment, I knew that no matter what obstacles we faced, I would always cherish the bond I shared with my child and hold onto the hope of reconciliation with my mother and Malik's family. Because I did not have anywhere to go to from the hospital,

Malik had to beg his parents to let me stay with them for some time until I reconciled with my family. While Malik's parents welcomed me and my first child with open arms, there lingered an unspoken tension born out of pity for my strained relationship with my own mother. After a few months, we became a big burden to Malik's parents, especially after I found out that I was pregnant again.

The strain of the second pregnancy and the mounting pressure from Malik's family proved to be too much for me and Malik's relationship to bear. Despite our love for each other, the weight of their circumstances became too heavy to carry, and we made the painful decision to part ways. With heavy hearts and tear-streaked faces, Malik and I said our goodbyes. We knew that breaking up was the best decision for both of us, but it didn't make it any easier to let go of the love we shared.

I returned to my parents' house, seeking refuge in the familiarity of my childhood home. But even there, I couldn't escape the pain of my shattered dreams and the lingering sense of loss that weighed heavily on my heart; and my mother did not make it any easier. I was not completely accepted back into the house; she made her home unpleasant to me and my child who she never accepted because she is bi-racial. And unfortunately, I was getting ready to have another mixed-race child.

In the days that followed, I focused on rebuilding my life and finding the strength to move forward. I started taking online classes to get my GED and see if I could find a job that would sustain me and my children. Most of my energy is poured into preparing for the arrival of my second child, determined to give them the love and support they deserved, even if it meant facing the challenges of single parenthood on my own because Malik went MIA on me. I tried to contact him to no avail; I went to his family and was told that he was relocated to a different state, apparently to avoid me and my children. His parents would ask to see my daughter every once in a while, but not him.

While all this was happening, one of my friends helped me get housing and food assistance while I was getting myself ready for a job. After I had my second child (a son), I started working and eventually got myself stabilized. I moved out of the project and started raising my children as a single mother.

As I adjusted to life as a single mother, the challenges of raising two young children on my own weighed heavily on my shoulders. With the demands of parenthood consuming my time and energy, I found myself longing for support and companionship.

In my search for solace, I found myself drawn to a Hispanic man, whose warmth and kindness offered me a sense of comfort I hadn't felt in a long time. As we spent more time together, our friendship blossomed into something more, and I found myself falling for his charm and charisma. But as our relationship deepened, my life took an unexpected turn when I discovered that I was pregnant once again, this time with a different man. The news sent shockwaves through my already fragile world, leaving me grappling with a whirlwind of emotions.

With no one else to turn to, I had to lean on the man who got me pregnant for support, finding solace in his unwavering presence by my side. Despite the challenges we faced, I clung to the hope that he would stand by me through thick and thin, offering me the love and support I so desperately needed.

My children faced a lot of prejudice and bullying at school and in society because of their skin color; I did not know how to make life easier for them but to start changing the way I see them to see if it would make it easy for them to fit in. My decision to present my mixed-race children as Caucasian stemmed from a place of deep pain and longing for acceptance, both from my mother and from society at large. I hoped that by concealing their true ethnicity, I could shield them from the prejudice and discrimination I had faced myself.

But as time passed with my children growing older, I began to realize the consequences of my actions. My children became confused about their true heritage, grappled with questions of identity, and belonging. They felt torn between the cultural identities that I had hidden from them and the truth that lay beneath the surface.

My oldest daughter started rebelling against how I was raising them and decided to get closer to her father's family despite the fact that her father has not been reaching out to her; her grandmother kept in touch with her. She made her understand that no matter what I am instilling in them, they should know that they are more African American than Caucasian.

I couldn't care less about my mother because I still blame her for all my misfortunes. If she had shown me love by loving our neighbors, I would have lived a better life. Even now that she is old and frail, she has not changed. She is still fighting people of color and people from different backgrounds. The worst part is that she has refused to accept my children, deepening the conflict between my mother and me.

How can I accept someone in my life who does not want to have anything to do with my children? The only child of mine that she tries to tolerate is my youngest daughter because she looks more Caucasian than mixed, and I went along with it, further confusing my child's heritage identity.

My mother tells me to my face that she regrets giving birth to me, that she would have had an abortion if she had known that I would grow up to be the way I am. She has cut me off, and I have cut her off as well. She told me that if I attend her funeral after she dies, she will turn in her casket; can you imagine a mother having that kind of hatred for her own child and grandchildren?

I have decided that I do not have a mother because I tried to make things right with her, but she refused to accept my mixed-race children, and she doesn't even hide the fact that she doesn't like and accept them. I have made my children understand that the only grandparents they have are Malik's parents, who have accepted them the way they are. So, I don't think that I would be able to care for her even if I want to because she would not want me to.

Caring for my mother would be like passing a camel through the needle's eye, meaning that it is very impossible and unlikely. She has already made plans for how she wants to be cared for and I believe that she has already signed up with a nursing home where she would be living during her last days, which is perfectly fine with me because she is very difficult to live with.

CHAPTER 17

Brenda's Account
Caring for My Elderly Uncle

My uncle raised me and my two brothers after our parents passed away and left us orphaned. When my father and his siblings were growing up, I was told that my uncle was like the black sheep of the family; nobody believed in him, nobody trusted him. My father was the only one in the family who had faith in my uncle. As a young man, he lived a reckless life. He played football and made a bunch of money doing that. He had three children with two different women whom he did not marry. Their parents never liked his way of life; he lived like there was no tomorrow. I remember when we were younger how he would come to our house to visit us, and my father would be advising him on how to live an upright life; he tried but was never lucky with women. He was very close to my father; they did a lot of things together.

I was about sixteen when my parents died in an auto accident. It was their wedding anniversary and my father had taken my mother to a classic restaurant to treat her. They were driving home when a drunk driver ran them off the road, and their car went over a bridge, killing both of them. Of course, the drunk driver was charged and locked up, but it did not bring my parents back. Since my brothers were older than me, I was the only one who had to go live with my uncle since he was the closest to my parents. It was not easy at first, but I got used to it and adapted to my new life. None of my uncle's children were living with him; they usually would come to visit him whenever they were allowed to.

I grew older, pursued my dreams, earned a college degree, and eventually found love. I married a kind-hearted man, and together, we started a family. Life seemed to be smiling upon me once again as I became a loving wife and mother to two beautiful children. However, fate had more twists in store for me as my once-rosy picture of my marriage started to fade; eventually, I found myself facing the painful reality of a divorce. Despite the challenges and heartbreak, I held onto the lessons of strength and resilience instilled in me by my uncle. He supported me during my divorce and helped me get back on my feet. I struggled as a single mother to raise my children, though I had my uncle who was always by my side to support my every effort.

With my children all grown and having their own families, I'm focused on my job now. My uncle, who is older and refuses to acknowledge that he is old, declined to move into an assisted living home. He was taking care of himself and living alone, which was not safe for him. I had to move in with him to be able to help him. My uncle and I shared stories, laughter, and tears. The roles had reversed, but the love and gratitude between us remained unwavering. My sacrifice was not just a duty; it was a testament to the enduring bond forged through years of shared joys and sorrows.

Caring for my uncle, I rediscovered the strength that had guided me through the storms of my own life. As the seasons changed and time marched forward, my commitment to my uncle remained steadfast. In this selfless act of love and gratitude, I found a renewed sense of purpose, and my uncle experienced the warmth of family when he needed it the most. Together, we embraced the journey of life's unpredictable chapters, finding solace in the enduring bonds of family that transcended the trials of time.

Despite my unwavering commitment to caring for my uncle out of love and gratitude, I faced harsh criticism from some of my relatives, particularly my uncle's children. They couldn't understand my selfless dedication and instead accused me of having ulterior motives. My uncle's children, who had distanced themselves from their father in his time of need, couldn't comprehend my willingness to sacrifice my own comfort and livelihood for the well-being of their father. They viewed my actions through a lens clouded by suspicion and selfishness, believing that I was only caring for my uncle to secure my inheritance once he passed away. Despite the hurtful accusations and judgment from my relatives, I remained steadfast in my resolve. I knew in my heart that my intentions were pure and fueled by the deep bond I shared with my uncle. I refused to let the doubts and negativity of others sway me from fulfilling my duty and honoring the love and support my uncle had given me throughout my life. I brushed aside the criticisms and focused on providing the best possible care for my uncle, just as he had done for me in my darkest days, tending to his needs with compassion and tenderness.

My uncle made a bunch of money when he was younger, had flashy cars, lived in a beautiful big house that he paid for in full. He never lacked anything except that he was very unlucky when it comes to relationships. He tried his best to take care of his properties, was always meticulous with them, and I helped him in caring for and managing his properties. This led some people to think that I was after his properties. He never neglected his children; he cared for them as much as he could until they were all grown and had their own families. He realized that despite being there for them, they did not want to be there for him when he needed them, instead, being solely interested in what they would gain from him.

One of his sons had a gambling problem and wanted to use one of his cars as collateral, which my uncle found out about and was understandably upset. This situation escalated tensions within the family, adding strain to our relationships. I bore much of the blame as it was believed that I had informed my uncle about his son's intentions. My cousins harbored resentment towards me, openly expressing their animosity and advising me to stay away from their father. However, despite the conflicts and hostility, I remained steadfast in showing love and care for my uncle.

As my uncle reached the remarkable age of 100, his health began to decline, signaling that his time on this earth was nearing its end. In our quiet moments together, he expressed his gratitude to me for the love and care I had provided him over the years. Realizing the significance of his remaining days, he made a decision that would reshape our family's legacy. With a clear mind and purpose, he composed his will, distributing his assets among his children, my brothers, and me, with a significant emphasis on favoring me. He wanted to prevent any disputes or quarrels among his children once he passed away. In his will, he elucidated the rationale for his choice, highlighting my dedicated care and unwavering commitment to his well-being as the core reasons behind his decision. He acknowledged my selflessness, my sacrifices, and the profound bond we shared—a bond that transcended blood relations and exemplified the true essence of family; he became the father figure I lost when I was sixteen.

My heart overflowed with emotion upon learning of his decision. I was deeply moved by this gesture, understanding it as a reflection of the gratitude he held towards me. More than that, it validated the deep bond we had nurtured—a connection forged through shared experiences of joy, sorrow, and steadfast support, embodying the unconditional love we harbored for each other. Caring for my uncle was a blessing, akin to caring for my parents had they been alive. Despite the challenges and obstacles, I do not regret a moment of it, and given the chance, I would willingly do it all over again.

CHAPTER 18

Clara's Account
Taking Care of a Loving Mother-in-law

When people say that first impression matters, I believe it, but sometimes first impression might be a way of someone trying to exercise some authority, power, or control. The first time I met my mother-in-law, I told my friends that I would not marry my husband because of the way she looked at me and treated me. I was going out with my husband for about eight months, and one day he decided that he would like for me to meet his parents. I was confused because I did not know what he was planning; he was not showing any sign of seriousness or commitment to our relationship. I eventually found out what had happened.

It was a late spring evening; his mother had invited him to come over to their house for dinner since he missed the family dinner that they had the previous week because he had a work engagement. He decided that it would be a great idea to introduce me to his parents. His father was on the quiet side, he did not talk much but likes to observe; his mother, on the other hand, liked to exercise authority. I don't know why, but for some reason, I was so nervous, and that is completely unlike me. When we got there, their house help came and opened the door for us. His mother came to the door, hugged him, completely ignored me with my pretty smile and warm heart.

He held my hand, and we went to their living room; his father was sitting there watching television. He went over to him, hugged him, and pulled me over so that his father would see me. His father smiled at me, shook my hand, and asked how I was doing. He was warm and kind; he welcomed me to their home and asked me to take a seat next to where he was sitting. Meanwhile, his mother was busy in the kitchen telling the help what to put on the dining table and what to pack up for her son. She made me feel invisible and small.

My husband kept asking if I was ok and that I should feel at home. I could not feel at home; honestly, I felt unwanted, unwelcomed, and needed to find an escape route. When she was done putting food on the table, she invited her husband and my husband to the dining. I sat where I was. My husband came to me and asked for me to get up and go to the dining with them, but I refused and told him that I was not hungry; he stated that it would be disrespectful if I did not eat with them, but I was thinking to myself how I could eat when I was not even welcomed.

His father, who was already seated and was dishing out his food, called out for me to come over and eat with them; I thanked him and told him that I was not hungry. That was when, for the first time, his mother recognized that there was another person in that house with them because she turned to me and said, "if you don't want to eat with us, then why did you come? Did my son not tell you that he was going to his parent's house?" I got up and went to eat with them. I was quiet all through the visit, even on our way from there. I kept telling myself that her behavior towards me just explained why her children are always trying to avoid her. So, tell me, who would want to marry into a family like that or who would like to have a woman like that as a mother-in-law.

After that incident, we became best friends; I

was skeptical when she started getting close to me. What happened was that my husband saw everything that happened but pretended like he did not see it. When he proposed to me, I told him that I would like to marry him, but because of his mother, that I would prefer that he marries somebody else who his mother would accept because I cannot marry a man who his mother does not like me.

A few days later, I got a phone call from his mother asking how I was doing and trying to carry on a conversation with me. She asked me what our plans were for our engagement party. Oh yes, she did! I opened my mouth to respond but was tongue-tied. We became so close that my husband and his siblings became jealous. When my father-in-law passed away, I was the first person that my mother-in-law called to tell what happened. I ran to be by her side; she cried on my shoulder like a baby. She was broken after her husband passed away; she became fragile, but her children were still seeing her as that strong authoritative, strict mother, and they treat her that way.

After her husband's funeral, we became even closer; it was hard to believe that someone who had treated me like a nobody previously would love me almost more than her own children. She started coming to visit us frequently to the point that my neighbors thought that she was my mother; they never knew that she was my mother-in-law. Then the unexpected happened. She started noticing changes in her bowel habit, started losing appetite, occasionally bloody stool, abdominal pain and cramp, consistent weakness, and weight loss without trying to lose weight.

She went to her primary care physician, and they ran some tests and gave her some medicines to ease her pain and help correct her bowel habit, but it did not help her problems. They eventually referred her to a gastroenterologist who after running some tests found out that she had colon cancer. I went with her when she went to talk to an oncologist; she held my hand so tight that I thought that my fingers would break by the time we leave the office. She was scared and anxious, and a little depressed since the day she was told her diagnosis. She would cry when no one was watching and put up a brave face when family was around. I was with her through all her treatments from chemotherapy to radiation to rehab; until the doctors gave us the news that we were expecting but did not want to hear it.

She stopped responding to treatment and needed to be on hospice care. I was broken because she had become my mother and my best friend. Who would have thought that we would be this close considering how she treated me the first time that she saw me at her house. She was taken to a hospice facility for a week, and she asked to be discharged to home hospice. She said that she would like to die in the comfort of her own home. When she came back home, my siblings-in-law and I were taking turns taking care of her. I would always go there to check on her whether it was my turn to care for her or not.

On this fateful day, it was my sister-in-law's day to stay with her and care for her that day; I went over in the morning to see how she was doing, that had been my routine since she was on home hospice. I would go there in the morning before going to work and go back to see her in the evening before going home for the day. When I left, I told her that I would see her that evening; she nodded ok. As soon as I got to work, my sister-in-law called my office phone number and said that she was trying my cell phone but could not get any response. My heart skipped a beat because I thought that she had died. She told me that my mother-in-law was asking to talk to me. I asked if they could put her on the phone, but she refused to talk to me over the phone. My boss at work was aware of our family situation, and she knew that I would be asking for off without warning due to my mother-in-law's condition. I went to her and told her that I had to leave to go be with my mother-in-law.

By the time I got to her house, everybody was already there. I started crying because of how they were all looking. My husband held me and took me to one of the rooms, calmed me down, and told me that she sent for all of them. We all went into the room where she was laying down. She looked at all of us and put up the most beautiful smile that I had ever seen.

I went over to where she was, hugged, and kissed her with tears in my eyes. She looked better than she was when I saw her that morning. I became scared because I knew that she was about to leave us. When I hugged her, she pulled me closer to her and whispered in my ear that she would like to talk to me alone; I nodded okay.

After everybody else left the room, I sat on her bed, very close to her. She raised her shaky hand and held my right hand; I turned to face her and held her shaky hand with both of my hands. She started thanking me for allowing her to be a mother to me and for being her daughter. She told me that she did not mean to, but she loved me more than her own children. She told me that she loved me from the very first day that she set her eyes on me and knew that I was right for her son.

She went ahead and said to me that she would like for me to take over her house and care for her children like they were my blood siblings. She made me promise to keep her family together and help them live in peace with each other. She asked me to help the family lawyer in distributing the family assets. By this time, I was boho crying; she wiped my tears and said that all was well and that she believed in me.

She gave me this last smile and put her head on my laps. I was rubbing her hand when I felt a cold chill all over me. I looked at her; she looked peaceful with her head on my laps when she took her last breath; she looked like she was sleeping. I could not figure out why she chose me out of all her children and her daughters-in-law.

I cried out so loud that everybody came running to me. I refused to get up from the bed. I refused for them to take her head off my laps. I felt like my world had shattered. It was an absolute blessing to know and be a part of this woman who became a mother and a best friend to me. I wish that I had more time to spend with her; her time with us felt so short.

My children had gotten attached to her; they loved her so much since they did not get to see their grandfather, and she adored them. Not just my children but all her grandchildren. I am grateful for the little time that I had with her and very glad that I did not judge her based on the first impression I had of her or the first experience that I had with her; I would have lost out on the blessings of knowing her real self, her kind and beautiful soul.

I loved her deeply and still do; I cannot talk
about her without having tears in my eyes.

Summarizing All of the Accounts

Going through these accounts made me see the elderly differently, and taking care of them, from my understanding, is mainly a blessing rather than a burden. You should treat people how you would like to be treated; try to see things from other people's perspectives. Always put yourself in other people's shoes and feel what they feel before you judge them or treat them unfairly.

I understand that there are accounts stating how some parents never cared about their children; however, the truth is, no matter how much you think they don't care, believe it or not, they do care about you. Due to our differences, we tend to express our love differently.

To children, adults, to anyone with living parents, grandparents, in-laws, uncles, aunties, cousins, and other relatives, please show them love. If there are any unresolved issues, try to mend them because life is short. Adding hate only contributes more stress to already stressful lives. Being kind doesn't take much; it can only add blessings to your already blessed life.

Parents, exhibit your love to your children, even when it becomes challenging to do so.

Disclaimer:

The stories in this book are work of fiction that depict true-life events, although modified to portray the significance of caring for our elderly when they can no longer care for themselves. The names used are fictional, created to spice up the stories. The individual stories written here were altered to fit in the real-life events that are happening in different communities. It is meant to convey the importance of caring for our loved ones.

www.ingramcontent.com/pod-product-compliance
Lightning Source LLC
Chambersburg PA
CBHW020439160726
48196CB00080B/8